5 EFFECTIVE TECHNIQUES TO CALM YOUR MIND

5 Effective Techniques to Calm Your Mind

A One Month Plan to Reduce Anxiety, Eliminate Negative Thinking & Build Healthy, Positive Habits for the Brain

SHANNON CORBYN

Contents

Introduction

The conversation surrounding mental health has become an increasingly popular topic in this country, and rightfully so. Around 40 million American adults suffer from common forms of anxiety disorder and related mental illnesses. With such high numbers and only 36% of those suffering receiving the necessary treatment, that leaves us with many people going about their daily lives, struggling to gain control over their own minds and emotions.

Many of us fall victim to the side effects that come with the very real and natural causes of anxiety, such as busy schedules and unhealthy sleeping and eating patterns. However, what we have been failing to see is that our own quality of life is dependent on how our minds process thoughts, events, and emotions.

Do you often feel as though you've struggled to remain motivated? Or constantly battle with yourself to accomplish everything that you need to? These are all symptoms of anxiety, along with other symptoms such as excessive worrying, mental fog, a short attention span or racing thoughts. When we start to normalize these cognitive symptoms within us, it then starts to seep into other aspects of our lives, such as physical symptoms: heart palpitations, insomnia, bursts of sweat, shortness of breath, nausea and excessive trembling. This can then affect our mood, leaving us feeling an impending sense of doom, fearful of the worst possible outcome, irritability and restlessness.

Naturally, the build-up of these feelings seeps further into our lives, negatively affecting our levels of productivity, motivation, eating and sleep habits, and most importantly, our ability to sustain healthy relationships. The worst outcome (if these symptoms persist without any active attention or change) is that our mental thought-patterns can lead to a decline in our overall physical health. Constantly experiencing high levels of stress, anxiety and negative thoughts can heighten risks of issues like obesity, diabetes, depression, gastrointestinal issues (such as Irritable Bowel Syndrome), heart disease and even Alzheimer's disease.

Our minds are one of the most complex organs to study. We've only recently come to understand how combinations of events and environments impact our mind, and then study how that impacts our lifestyle and overall quality of life. What's worse is that as we normalize the habit of entertaining such negative thoughts and feed into our anxiety, we are actually giving it the power to control and run our life for us. In doing so, we can lose control of our thoughts, emotions and situations.

However, the good news is that the discussion for mental health awareness *is* now broadening and growing in popularity. We have finally been able to study the effects that our mental health and thought processes can have on our lives, and spot direct relations between the two.

In *5 Effective Techniques to Calm Your Mind*, we will be exploring natural and healthy ways to adjust smaller (yet impactful) mental habits, so that we can make room for healthier, happier and more productive versions of ourselves! With five simple techniques, we will explore how to completely reprogram your thought patterns and thought processes with habits that you can practice daily, for long-lasting and life-changing effects!

We don't need to let the situation get out of hand before we seek medical help—the change can start right now, in our own homes and in our own minds. Join us as we explore the techniques to become more aware of our emotions, feelings and most importantly, our triggers, so that we can find constructive and healthy ways of regaining control over these aspects in a healthy and productive manner. Not only will we regain control over our thoughts, emotions and situations, we will also be reducing levels of anxiety and stress as well as heightening our quality of living, all in five easy-to-remember categories.

Many people who have followed these simple steps have thanked me for how they have positively changed their lives using the tools to reduce anxiety and negative thought patterns. As we explore them in this book, you too can have these daily techniques at your disposal!

Why Choose This Book?

It is very important to understand and become more aware of the emotion of anxiety, as many of the articles you can find on the Internet don't go into detail about their source, leaving the reader struggling to learn how to recognize them. By contrast, through this book, you can learn how to trace and treat the root causes of anxiety, so that you can learn to evaluate, observe, and make these changes with practical examples and techniques.

You should choose this book if you are a person who is struggling to deal with negative and anxious emotions, and you would like to understand how they work in your brain. Moreover, if you want to know how to recognize these anxious and negative thoughts when they creep into your mind, and finally apply practical methods to eliminate them and reduce anxiety, then this is the book for you.

By the end of this read, you will know how to identify negative and anxious emotions and the causes and more importantly, you will be better equipped to deal with them.

Within the first two chapters, we will be discussing and exploring what negative thinking and anxiety are, how they're interconnected, what effect they have on our lives, and most importantly, how to spot and identify these elements. The first step toward growth and progress is to become conscious of unhealthy habits which we normalized. Only then can growth and healing take place. After this, we will move onto exploring how to replace these elements within our thought-processes with much more constructive and healthy factors.

In the following chapters, you and I will be exploring some of the most powerful and efficient techniques to help you:

1. Identify your negative thoughts, negative beliefs, and/or negative thought patterns.
2. Discover the causes of several forms of anxiety disorder and their symptoms.
3. Identify the habits of cognitive distortions.

4. Train your brain to think more positively and rationally to combat negative thinking and anxiety.
5. Break bad habits and adopt new constructive habits.

Techniques which we will explore include the power that affirmations have and how to properly use them. After that, we will explore more of the technical side of self-talk and mental maps—this includes exploring neuro-linguistic programming and cognitive behavioural therapy. Exploring these terms and their forms of therapy can help us further reprogram our minds to become more efficient and think more rationally without wasting too much emotional energy! We will then move onto a more light-hearted topic: ways to efficiently calm the mind and work on positive, uplifting habits to adopt. In those sections, we will be covering topics such as meditation, mindfulness and other healthy habits to keep your mind, energy and body well sustained, so that you can tackle your days as optimally as possible.

The tools that we will explore within this book are going to equip you to tackle not only the larger events in your life, but your normal day-to-day living. As cliché as it may sound right now, change doesn't happen overnight. What you will uncover are ways to reprogram your mind to practice daily positive thinking habits, so as to promote long-lasting and life-changing results!

Your Free Bonus

To help my readers to achieve the best result while you are implementing the techniques in the book, I have created a list of all the useful and effective tools to help you along the way. Make sure you type this link to access https://bit.ly/3vNHsHi, or email me at shannoncorbyn@gmail.com with title "Calm your mind", and I'll send you the bonus!

Chapter 1

Identifying our Negative Thoughts

"A mind grows by what it feeds on."

· J.G. Holland

Through the current conversation surrounding mental health, we can understand how the power of our own mind can affect our perception of our world, as well as create and enhance factors in the world on which we place our focus on. And as the saying goes, "with great power comes great responsibility." We similarly need to be very responsible in treating our mental health.

As J.G Holland suggests, we create the literal world in which we give interest. When we entertain negative thoughts, they not only affect our mood and energy levels, they also start to paint a mirage of a world stemming from those negative thoughts. What's worse is that our brain loves to connect things together and thrives off of muscle memory, so the more that we subconsciously entertain negative thoughts and allow them to dictate our perception of our world, the more we experience them. Thus we fall into a vicious cycle of feeling constantly depressed, anxious, angry and unmotivated. It feels as though nothing we do is enough, we may feel a lack of control over what happens to us and a lack of control over our own emotions. Overall, we feel a lesser sense of power and control within our own lives.

Once you've caught yourself stuck in this loop of uncontrollability, it may seem as if there's no winning and your sense of self degrades. This cycle is known as our 'automatic negative thoughts' (ANTs). It's a constant habit of entertaining negative thoughts that seep into other factors of your life, from your moods to your habits, levels of productivity, problem solving and managing relationships (Learn to Identify Automatic Negative Thoughts, 2019).

"Negative thinking is thinking that leads to negative consequences."

· Dr. Steven M. Melemis

Understandably, these ANTs greatly impact our lives in a negative way; however, it must be noted that if our minds have the power to dictate our life in a certain way, it can just as easily be trained to perceive our life in another more positive and productive way. This process is considered "cognitive behavioral therapy" (CBT) (Smith, n.d.). CBT essentially promotes the idea and provides methods of reprogramming our minds to swap out ANTs with more positive and uplifting thoughts by challenging our minds to view scenarios as a bigger picture and not see everything in black-and-white. In doing so, we're essentially training our minds to look at all factors of a scenario and consider some of the positive factors, attributes and lessons from them, rather than placing the power of the scenario in the hands of your emotions and believing that you are the victim in every scenario. ANTs also come in the form of excuses, as opposed to taking the necessary actions and learning from experience.

In this book, we will be uncovering the ways to go about training and reprogramming our minds through CBT techniques to achieve that higher sense of self, while eliminating ANTs and reducing levels of anxiety. Still, the first step to any form of healing is to be able to understand and identify the problem before we can explore the solutions. Therefore, before striving for solutions, we will need to fully explore and understand ANTs as well as truthfully identify our own ANTs.

Understanding "Negative Thinking"

Managing our responsibilities while achieving a wholesome and balanced lifestyle can be an overwhelming task. Entertaining negative thoughts and thought patterns can gradually add to our levels of anxiousness, and leave us feeling completely over-whelmed.

Unfortunately, it is all too easy to fall into a vicious cycle of entertaining the negative thoughts that feed into our levels of anxiety, while forcing ourselves to silence the symptoms that come from the illness. In doing so, we've normalized extremely high levels of stress, heart palpitations, irregular sleeping patterns, digestive issues, a lack of control over our emotions, and mental fog, thus leading to an overall decline in quality of life.

Considering that negative thinking and negative thought patterns can fuel anxiety, we should aim to become much more aware of how often it happens. The issue with this is that because these habits aren't always immediately physically present, it can be much harder to identify them and change them. It's only once these habits of negative thinking manifest themselves physically, causing demotivation, laziness, mental fog, struggles with sleep cycles, etc. that we start to notice the need for change.

Before we move on to working on how to identify these negative thinking patterns, we need to first understand *what* exactly negative thinking and negative thought patterns are. For those of you who tend to overthink, it may be a bit tougher to identify what are negative thoughts and what aren't.

Now, when we refer to "negative thoughts," we

aren't necessarily referring to normal emotional reactions to daily life. For instance, if you've just found out that your pet has fallen ill, you are allowed to experience sadness and worry over your pet's health and their medical bills. These emotions and thoughts are completely normal and part of our system of processing events.

The main difference between what we consider human nature and what we consider "negative thinking" is the persistence and repetition of negative thoughts. When these thoughts start to pop up repeatedly in our minds or in conversations with others, we then need to evaluate the importance that we're placing on these thoughts. We need to start questioning how productive these thoughts are, whether these thoughts are helping us progress forward and think clearly, or whether we entertain these thoughts as excuses to self-limit ourselves.

When referring to negative thinking, we are often looking at the patterns of negative thoughts. The major points of concern are negative thoughts that revolve around yourself or your surroundings. This could be an emotional surrounding such as a group of people, or it could be a physical surrounding, such as your workplace (Smith, n.d.).

The weight of "negative thinking" in your life is completely dependent on how seriously it affects you. Whether you experience and entertain patterns of negative thoughts every now and then, or allow the negative thoughts to debilitate you (emotionally, mentally or even physically), these strings of negative thoughts can fuel your levels of anxiety and hinder your ability to function optimally.

More importantly, negative thinking doesn't necessarily mean that *everyone* who entertains habits of negative thinking has a mental illness. Although negative thinking can be a contributing factor towards worsening symptoms of mental health (such as anxiety, depression, and personality disorders), negative thinking can also exist on its own or be a bridge toward other mental illnesses—that's what makes it so sneaky and subtle, yet powerful. By raising our awareness of these habits, we can then take a step in the right direction of healing and relieving symptoms of mental illnesses, as well as growing emotionally, mentally and even physically in a positive manner.

RECOGNIZING THE PATTERNS

When analyzing thoughts which you may feel are negative or hindering your ability to think clearly or function optimally, you can ask yourself one or more of the following questions:

- Is this thought 100% truthful, or is there a bias that's influencing this thought? For instance, if you have constantly shied away from public speaking, you may encounter patterns of negative thinking in relation to doing presentations at work or speaking up in meetings, because you may feel that you lack the confidence and skill.

You may have developed this bias towards your ability to speak publicly, thus leave you in a position where you may even decline job offers or fantastic opportunities due to this fear.

· Is the thought giving you power or taking power away from you? As mentioned in the previous example, you may be removing power from yourself (through a lack of self-belief) and limiting your own ability to tackle situations with self-confidence.

· Can you turn this negative thought to a positive one, or can you learn anything from your negative thoughts? For instance, instead of saying "I'm not good at public speaking," you can change this to "I will work on my public speaking skills until I'm comfortable and confident enough to speak publicly." Alternatively, you can aim to question *why* you've placed a limit on yourself and then question what you can learn from this experience. For instance, if you've had terrible public speaking experiences in the past, you can aim to figure out how to work around the situation to benefit you without limiting yourself. For instance, you can provide more digital content at a presentation (such as videos, graphs, etc.) to support your points and guide your speaking. Alternatively, you could find ways to better your public speaking abilities by taking classes—the options for this scenario are endless!

- Ask what your life would be like if your negative thoughts were nonexistent. How different would your life be? Would you live your life more freely? If so, this can indicate that these thought patterns need to be worked on, so as to reduce the stress and anxiety that it's placing on your mind and body.

- The last question is most likely one of the most important of questions to ask yourself: is the negative thought or negative thought pattern existing to gloss over a much bigger issue that needs to be addressed? For instance (in keeping with the public speaking example), is the pattern of negative thoughts stemming from a deeper-rooted issue? This could, for example, be from trauma in relation to a public speaking incident that went wrong in the past. Aim to question *why* you have negative thoughts in relation to this issue and if you need to fix a bigger, deeper-rooted issue. It's pointless that we work towards eliminating negative thoughts if we're overlooking the root cause of them. Once we are able to identify that cause, we can then work to heal that area and then reprogram our minds correctly to handle those scenarios.

For example, if you do have trauma from a public speaking incident gone wrong, we can then focus on how to heal from that scenario and understand that that one specific incident does not define us (compared to the power that we give it). We can then work towards how to overcome that fear in a healthy way and most importantly, grow from it and learn from it.

In addition to these key questions, you can also consider becoming more aware of thinking patterns that give way to negative spirals (Sey, n.d. pg. 16-17).

- Entertaining negative self-talk or negative self-labelling.
- Possessing an inability or unwillingness to acknowledge the positive factors within yourself or a situation.
- Having an excessive need for approval or validation from others.
- Trying to get into the minds of others and assuming that they think the worst of you.
- Excessively dwelling on negative aspects of yourself to the point that you begin to consider those aspects to be defining points within yourself.

These traits may be much easier to spot than the aforementioned internal negative thinking examples, as they provide more tangible proof of negative thinking (such as requiring an excessive amount of validation from others). These characteristics can be prevalent in our conversations with others, which makes them much easier to point out and adjust accordingly. However, characteristics of negative thinking stem from negative thoughts, so if you are noticing these characteristics arise, you can treat these as signifiers of subconscious negative thinking habits which we will need to work on as we progress with this book.

ANT TYPES

As studies of negative thinking developed over the years, psychiatrists such as Aaron Beck and David Burns began offering newer terms for behaviours that we often deal with, to then help us identify with different aspects of negative thinking.

Because our minds are such a vast and complex thing to grasp and understand, these terms and types of negative thinking can help us better understand how our minds work and most importantly, work towards efficiently healing from these negative thought processes (Sey, n.d. pg. 18-21).

Author of "Positive Thinking," Ralph Sey, suggests that there are 'types' of negative thinking and characteristics that can influence our behaviour. Psychiatrists such as Beck and Burns (among others) had proposed this relation between negative thinking and cognitive behaviour as early as the 1960s. Nowadays, we refer to this as "cognitive distortions." Cognitive distortions shouldn't be viewed as anything negative nor should it cause any level of stress or worry; the term simply exists to provide a term for the effect which may come with negative thinking, and aids us in understanding how to tackle the effects of negative thinking.

The first and most prominent type of negative thinking and cognitive distortion is to hold a strong belief that our feelings drive our behaviour. A clear example of this is to postpone taking action on something until you feel good, *rather than* believing that doing that action will make you feel good. For instance, if you have a goal in mind, surely meeting those targets to achieve that goal would feel good, right? However, at the moment, we can often be tempted by laziness and cave into procrastinating. We give into our feelings for that instant gratification while sacrificing that feeling of accomplishment. How often do we tend to say the phrase "it can wait until tomorrow" or "it can wait another day," and fool ourselves into taking three times longer to achieve what we wanted to achieve? Finding excuses and procrastinating against our own better judgement is an extremely sneaky form of negative thinking, as it can hinder our ability to function as optimally as we'd like to!

Another important term to note is 'filtering'. As the term suggests, the act of filtering is to essentially filter out all other factors within a scenario and excessively focus on one (often insignificant) detail. Filtering can also be referred to as 'magnification' or 'minimization' as we give less or more power to specific factors within a scenario (Learn to Identify Automatic Negative Thoughts, 2019). Often, we create an entire opinion just by filtering a scenario. Filtering can also have immense power in determining our mood or our perception of a scenario. For instance, if you had a really fantastic time on a date but accidentally knocked over a glass of water towards the end of the date, you may only focus on that aspect and determine that the date went horribly and may even assume that your date is now uninterested in you or thinks that you're a klutz—essentially, making a minor and insignificant detail determine the success of the date as well as your feelings towards each other.

A more common phrase used is the term "jumping to conclusions"; this phrase ties in quite well with filtering and can go hand-in-hand with filtering scenarios. When we jump to conclusions, we're essentially creating a false idea of the reason that something happened (or creating a hypothetical conclusion) without considering the bigger picture and all of the factors involved. For instance, you could think that your date is now not interested in going on another date with you because you dropped a glass of water. You haven't taken into consideration all of the other factors: the date went well, you got along with your date and had fun, you share a lot of common interests with your date, etc.

"Polarized thinking" and 'shoulds' are two categories that can also be quite detrimental to our perception of events. Polarized thinking suggests that there is no grey area, that everything needs to be one way or another. 'Shoulds' refers to a belief that there is no room for excuses and that everyone should be following the same set of societal rules without room for compromise. These categories can tie in with the distortion of 'needing to be right.' You may feel as though your opinion is battling with other opinions that 'oppose' it, when in reality, you may just need to find a compromise.

'Personalization' pertains to believing that you're the center of every scenario, and that everything that happens is about you. This is related to "jumping to conclusions" and can also lead to quite a lot of anxiety. For instance, if someone is too busy to give you attention, you feel as though it has something to do with you. You may start to think that you did something to them that caused them to distance themself from you or that they simply don't like interacting with you, when in fact, they're merely just too busy to give you attention at that point in time.

The last category is broken up into three aspects of fallacy: control fallacies, fallacy of fairness and reward fallacies. Control fallacy is similar to personalization in the sense that you feel as though everything revolves around you; however, control fallacy relates to the feeling that you are responsible for everyone else's happiness and fall victim to factors that are out of your control. The fallacy of fairness suggests a feeling of bitterness that results from an expectation not being met. Lastly, the reward fallacy suggests that you expect there to always be a tangible reward for the work that you put in, causing you to get upset if the work isn't acknowledged. This can be extremely de-motivating, as it suggests that you are chasing goals for the rewards, rather than the actual achievement (of the work put in and the lessons and skills that are learned along the way). As cheesy as it may sound, the reward fallacy stands for the direct opposite idea of "enjoying the journey, not the destination." You may feel so caught up in striving for the reward that whether or not your actions may be recognized, you completely lose sight of the valuable lessons along the way.

By shedding light and raising our level of awareness of mental habits like the ones mentioned above, we can then move onto understanding how these aspects feed into our levels of anxiety. Once we realize the weight that we've given to these mental habits, then we can start to realize the true impact that these habits are leaving in our lives; only then will we be able to make the necessary changes to combat the true effects of negative thoughts.

EXPLORING WHAT CAN TRIGGER AN ANT

When we refer to 'triggers,' we are referring to an element that sets off your ANTs. Trigger elements can come in any form—physical interaction, verbal communication, encounters, scenarios, etc. Triggers are anything that sparks an irrational or excessive re-sponse to the situation at hand, thus causing us to think (and often respond) in an irrational way. This can be quite detrimental for our own health because we're allowing these triggers to constantly affect us and in turn, we're giving our power, emotion and energy into a situation in an unproductive manner. By spotting our triggers and even exploring *why* we react to these triggers, we can then move onto exploring and training our minds to handle the encounters with these triggers in the most productive and least stressful manner.

Triggers for ANTs and types of ANTs can go hand-in-hand. For instance, we may have a thought that causes us to "jump to conclusions," which could then lead to us normalizing that ANT type as a mode of thinking in stressful scenarios. Say, for example, that you were presenting at a meeting and you started to believe that the clients' facial expressions suggested that they were uninterested in your pitch. You may jump to conclusions within the pitch and start to doubt the content that you were presenting. This may trigger your anxiety and have you doubting yourself or your work without hearing the client's feedback.

One of the major triggers for ANTs is overthinking or overanalyzing a scenario, as this can lead to your mind trying to reason with false images or thoughts that are now implanted in your mind—images and thoughts that don't consider the bigger picture.

Other forms of triggers can be more physically prevalent, such as neglecting aspects of your physical health or facing changes to balanced physical health, ie. sleep deprivation or inconsistent sleeping patterns, irregular eating habits, exhaustion, constant overexposure to high levels of stress (such as constantly facing stressful environments), and even times when we're feeling sick or suffering from allergies. These are a few of the more prominent issues that can affect our mood and leave us spiralling into a cycle of negative thought patterns. If you experience one or more of them, consider trying to bring more balance to your lifestyle or balancing your mental health out by creating a habit of practicing positive affirmations. In doing so, you're allowing your body, emotions, mind and spirit to set aside the ANTs and force it to focus on positive parts of your life. In turn, you're relieving your body and mind from its pent-up stress.

Other triggers for ANTs can come in the form of biases which you've created over years of a specific experience. It's important to note that if we can work towards identifying our triggers as well identifying how we react to those triggers (such as specific ANTs, anxiousness, disrupted sleep, heart palpitations, sadness, etc.) we can then combat these triggers and effects with more direct and specific solutions. For instance, if you know that you struggle with public speaking and you have a constant fear that you'll mess up because it has happened to you in the past, you can then work towards combating th0se specific ANTs. The more specific you are when identifying ANTs and their triggers, the easier it will be to reprogram your mind to identify them and replace them with positive thoughts!

Chapter 2

Understanding Anxiety and Anxiety Disorders

Considering that over 40 million American adults suffer from some form of anxiety, and the fact that negative thinking can be directly related to these effects, it's important that we explore the issue of anxiety and identify what elements of anxiety we may be experiencing. In doing so, we can work towards relieving ourselves of the effects of the disorder, rather than normalizing it and worsening the effects that it has over us.

It's important to understand that anxiety is a normal emotion that we all face every now and then. However, if we expose ourselves to it much too often, it can start to hinder our ability to think and act rationally (which then leads into cognitive behavioral disorder). High levels of anxiety can also become a medical disorder and lead to other illnesses and diseases such as depression, irritable bowel syndrome or heart disease.

While the term 'anxiety' refers to a normal, human emotion that we all face, 'anxiety disorder' pertains to those that experience anxiety at disproportionate levels and can often leave one feeling mentally, emotionally and sometimes even physically crippled by the overwhelmingly high and constant levels of anxiety (Felman, 2020). Anxiety disorder can also trigger feelings of excessive nervousness, fear, apprehension and worry. Other feelings which anxiety disorder can trigger is a feeling of impending doom, an inability to stay calm and still, and a heightened level of uneasiness.

Physical symptoms of anxiety disorder can leave one feeling nauseous or issues with their digestive system (such as cramping, inconsistencies in stool, vomiting), excessive sweating, heart palpitations, lightheadedness and shortness of breath. Some that suffer from anxiety disorder can also experience trembling or tense muscles and tingling in their hands and feet. Hyperventilating is also quite common with anxiety disorder and can be triggered much faster.

Overall, anxiety disorder can distort your ability to see things clearly and make clear judgements on scenarios, as you're constantly battling with the emotional and physical symptoms that come with the disorder. One may struggle to concentrate fully at the moment, while simultaneously ruminating over negative thoughts or fears. The 'filtering' ANT type can also come into play in this case, as one may spend their time hyper focusing on one specific, negative factor and struggle to see the bigger picture of the scenario.

Anxiety disorder, if left untreated, can also seep into other aspects of your life. For instance, anxiety disorder can affect your eating and sleeping cycles. Some may struggle to eat at all, while others tend to overeat during stressful periods. Some may feel completely fatigued and oversleep while others struggle to fall asleep and neglect their quality of sleep (Julson, 2018). Sleep disturbances, restlessness and insomnia are extremely common for those that suffer with anxiety disorder.

Some of the more disabling forms of anxiety disorder can become more prevalent or triggered by social settings—such as having panic attacks, difficulty concentrating or avoiding social situations altogether.

Panic attacks are definitely something of concern if you do suffer from anxiety disorder as they can be recurring, intense and debilitating. Recurring panic attacks are referred to as "panic disorder" and come in the form of rapid heartbeat/heart palpitations, sweating, shaking, shortness of breath, nausea and chest tightness. During this period, you may literally start to feel and think as though you're dying, or at least experience the fear of death. Although panic disorder isn't as common, it's still worth noting that anxiety disorder can fuel a panic attack. Similarly, the trauma after experiencing a panic attack can also cause one to feel anxious about experiencing another one in the future.

Social situations have been less prevalent recently, considering the pandemic that we are living through; this has worked in favour of those who experience social anxiety. However, socializing and interacting is a human's natural need, and those that suffer from social anxiety and lean towards isolating themselves are neglecting this very important aspect that helps bring a higher level of quality to life. Those that suffer from social anxiety disorder may experience anxiety and fear leading up to a social event, they may fear judgement or humiliation from others, or completely avoid social events altogether in fear that no one will want to interact with them. The mere idea of interacting with people may just trigger that anxiety altogether.

It's also important to mention within this section that phobias (irrational fears of something specific, such as spiders or heights) can also trigger our levels of anxiety and hinder us from functioning normally. If you are aware of any phobias of yours, you can also consider how you react in these situations and consider how to make yourself more comfortable in those situations to help reduce the levels of anxiety.

Ultimately, although we have come to understand how broad and common the effect of anxiety is within us, it's important that we aim to identify what types of anxiety affect us, how we react to it, what triggers it and how ANTs can contribute towards these levels of anxiety. In doing so, we can then gain a clearer understanding of the effects of anxiety on our emotions, bodies and energy levels. Then, we can then work towards reprogramming and preparing our minds and bodies to handle these situations much better, so that we're able to function as optimally, healthily and productively as possible.

Why Do We Get Anxious?

Understandably, 'anxiety' is a common emotion which we all possess. It's an emotion which we all experience and face. It's as normal of an emotion as any other that we experience, such as happiness and excitement, and it's an emotion that is necessary for balance within our lives. Feeling anxious isn't necessarily a bad thing, it only becomes a problem once it starts to control our ability to live our lives the way that we'd like.

For instance, if you experience a constant lack of concentration and struggle sleeping, you may start to get agitated and become mentally foggy, thus affecting your quality of work and life. If you experience effects of anxiety disorder such as a constant, impending sense of doom, you may become emotionally and mentally distanced from the present scenarios at hand.

You may also experience lower self-esteem or start to entertain negative self-talk, isolate yourself from social events, and you may even start to hypothesize the worst case scenario happening. All of these incidents work hand-in-hand with ANT and feed off of your fears to keep you stuck in a cycle that turns anxiety from a mere emotion into a full-blown disorder.

So the question is now, how does anxiety go from a mere emotion to a mental health issue? There are a few points that can trigger the emotion into becoming a powerful monster, but the essence of the development lies within the notion that those that experience an overexposure of anxiety, so that it builds up and becomes a disorder. One could argue that it's likely due to the fact that we start to normalize anxiety so much without working through it, that it eventually evolves into the overpowering disorder. The lack of balancing this emotion with other emotions and positive thoughts in combination with traumas, medical factors or even lifestyle habits all amalgamates to the development of the disorder.

Naturally, one of the first factors to consider in relation to anxiety disorder is genetics (Browne, 2020). Those that have family members who suffer from anxiety or anxiety disorder are more likely to experience some form of the disorder themselves. In keeping with this theme, medical factors and chemical imbalances in the brain are two other factors which could lead to the development of anxiety disorder. If, for instance, you take strong medication or undergo an intense surgery, anxiety disorder can be triggered from the stress placed on the body. Chemical imbalances or misalignment of hormones can also play a role in turning anxiety into a disorder.

Substance abuse as well as withdrawal from substances can also trigger anxiety due to the chemical imbalances in the brain. It's also important to note here that some use substances to cope with their anxiety, so naturally, withdrawal from it can lead to an overwhelming amount of anxiety.

One of the major points worth addressing is past events or traumatic experiences. However we manage to cope from these experiences, they can still continue to trigger us for years to come. However, it's vitally important to face these incidents, address them, and then heal and grow from them. Suppressing memories or emotions from these events can lead to pent-up anxiety, which can turn into major internal/subconscious stress, thus leading to anxiety disorder and ANTs.

Lastly, environmental stressors such as relationship issues or workplace issues can also place immense stress on us. A prime example of a vicious cycle of anxiety passed on to others would be a parent who carries their anxiety from work back to the family at home, lashing out at their children due to their higher rates of irritability and stress. Thus leaving both the parent and child dealing with high levels of anxiety from the workplace and the home environment. Unfortunately, this example is quite a common one, although the trending conversations around mental health have raised awareness in many to better handle their levels of anxiety, rather than pass it on.

All of the factors mentioned above can also be further triggered by lifestyle choices/habits such as unhealthy or irregular eating and sleeping patterns. Naturally, the stress that you face with anxiety disorder will make you want to neglect other considerably healthier aspects of your life (such as having balanced meals or exercising). These are completely normal feelings—some may even struggle to get out of bed in the morning. The most important way to heal from this is to identify and acknowledge these feelings before moving onto regaining those levels of motivation.

Types of Anxiety

There are several forms of anxiety disorder that are currently recognized and diagnosable in the Diagnostics and Statistical Manual of Mental Health Disorders: Fifth Edition (DSM-V) (Browne, 2020).

The first and most common form is Generalized Anxiety Disorder (GAD). GAD is not triggered by anything specific, but can cause immense anxiety and worry over long periods of time. GAD can also be rooted in genetics—if, for instance, there's a history of anxiety disorder that runs within the family.

Panic disorder, as we covered, comes with intense physical symptoms such as dizziness, nausea, and shortness of breath. Some panic attacks can cause one to faint from distress and can last anywhere between 10 minutes to hours at a time. They are usually triggered by prolonged periods of exposure to high stress environments/situations, but those that suffer from panic disorder can also suffer from spontaneous panic attacks without a trigger. Those that experience panic attacks may also generate more anxiety and stress after experiencing a panic attack because they are such traumatic experiences. Some feel as though the experience can be life-threatening or may worry that the panic attacks are a symptom of another more serious and life-threatening illness, so they may become more anxious to experience another in the future—causing more anxiety.

Phobias also fall under types of anxiety disorders which you can experience, although these are more specific to objects or situations, therefore can be identified and managed more easily. Encountering triggers for your phobia can range from sporadic events to everyday encounters, therefore the intensity of the phobia or the anxiety that's triggered from it can also range.

Avoiding situations, places, people or events is known as 'Agoraphobia' and can often leave one feeling trapped. Many people that suffer from agoraphobia often find it debilitating, in the sense that they fear encountering certain scenarios so they simply try their hardest not to encounter those scenarios. For instance, if someone fears public transportation, they may try to work around it so that they have to use public transport as little as possible. In this context, we can also consider social anxiety disorder or social phobia (which was covered in the previous section). This is where one may feel anxious towards social interaction and tend to isolate themselves or become extremely nervous around groups of people.

On the opposite end of the spectrum, there's separation anxiety disorder, whereby one may experience anxiety from being separated from a place or a person that they feel safe with. This person may affiliate this place/person as a comfort zone for them and being separated from this safe zone could trigger fear and panic.

Medication-induced anxiety disorder is the after-effects of withdrawal from certain medicines or illegal drug use. These withdrawal symptoms can trigger one to feel anxious, panicky and high levels of unease. It can also resort to the person experiencing agitation and even a fear that they may not be able to cope much longer without the intake of the drug/medication.

Disorders such as "obsessive-compulsive disorder" (OCD) and post-traumatic stress disorder (PTSD) once fell under the category of anxiety disorders in the DSM. However, in the fifth edition, OCD and PTSD aren't categorized under anxiety. It is important to note that these disorders can still trigger levels of anxiety within us and work hand-in-hand with anxiety disorder. OCD and PTSD can also be triggered by similar incidences as anxiety disorder. For instance, PTSD is triggered by a traumatic event and agoraphobia can be as well.

DO I HAVE AN ANXIETY PROBLEM?

As mentioned before, being able to identify our anxiety type, cause, and trigger can greatly assist us in bettering our quality of life.

When exploring a few of the types of anxiety, one of the easiest ways to spot whether you may be experiencing that type of anxiety is through its cause or through its symptoms. For instance, medication-induced anxiety is caused by withdrawal of medication or illegal drug use, and symptoms may show in the form of extreme unease, heart palpitations, breaking out in sweat, and general feelings of anxiousness and dizziness.

In this section, we will be further breaking down a few of the causes and symptoms of each of the types of anxiety disorder to assist you in determining whether or not you suffer from anxiety disorder. We will also be exploring the effects of living with these disorders so that one can even attempt to identify the after-effects of anxiety disorder in the quality of their lives.

The first type which we explored was GAD. Due to this type being so broad in regards to its triggers and causes, it depends more so on the person suffering from the disorder to investigate their own personal triggers or how to combat the symptoms of the disorder when they arise (often this can be unprovoked). With GAD, you can investigate a few aspects: whether anxiety disorder runs in your family, whether you've encountered a traumatic event (and processed it), whether you experience constant high levels of stress from environments or work, how balanced your diet and lifestyle is, etc. These factors could be a few scenarios that can spark GAD if left untreated. Alternatively, you can look at the symptoms of GAD to see if you identify with those: nausea, trembling, digestive issues, negative thoughts, issues with sleep cycles, shortness of breath, a constant feeling of worry, etc.

If you suffer from GAD, you'll tend to overthink many situations and encounters. You'll feel drained, lethargic, demotivated and constantly stressed from consistent overthinking. Your overall quality of life may be compromised with GAD, as you become more hesitant to act upon opportunities and even move at a much slower pace than you'd like to, because of the constant need to overthink as well as constantly needing to tackle the anxiety that comes with each encounter or scenario. Naturally, the buildup of the symptoms from GAD can lead to other illnesses and disorders. One of the main illnesses correlated with GAD is depression. You can also expect to see a stagnancy or decline in your quality of life, as you may struggle to find the motivation or energy to bring balance into your life through healthy sleeping and eating habits, socializing, exploring hobbies, etc. Some even refer to anxiety as a slow killer, because it's such a subtle yet powerful force that eats away at your quality of life, in all senses of the phrase—from your relationships to your work life, home life as well as your physical and mental health.

If you notice that you're lacking the ability to muster up the motivation, energy and confidence to go about your day while still being able to properly look after yourself, and you notice that you're experiencing a few other symptoms related to anxiety, which includes ANTs, then you may be experiencing some level of GAD.

Panic disorder can be noticeable to others if one suffers from it, considering the physical and debilitating symptoms that come with it. Panic attacks can leave one feeling completely out of control of their own levels of anxiety for hours on end, and thus can also lead to the development of other physical illnesses or diseases. Considering that panic attacks can physically, emotionally and mentally debilitate you for hours on end, panic disorder (especially if left untreated) has the potential to cause damage to our body and organs. It's important that if you do experience periods of panic attacks that you see a doctor for proper treatment of the disorder. In addition to this, you'll need to try and identify what factors could be triggering your panic attacks. One of the most important factors to consider is how often you entertain negative thinking and negative self-talk as these can be prompts for anxiety to be triggered. You may also need to consider dietary factors, sleep cycles, your stress management and stress levels as well as if any forms of mental health issues run in your family.

Phobias are also quite easy to spot if you notice that you have a specific fear towards something such as heights. Causes of phobias can stem from PTSD from previous negative encounters with the phobia or simply stem from the creation of negative hypothetical scenarios. For instance, you fear heights because you're scared that you may fall and hurt yourself. In doing so, you're hindering your ability to explore and experience life freely, as well as causing yourself a great deal of unnecessary stress and anxiety. Phobias can also hinder our ability to learn from our experiences, thus resulting in us caving into fear from hypothetical outcomes. It can debilitate us in the form of completely avoiding situations altogether, or the phobia can also have the power to leave us inoperable of our own mind and body when facing that phobia head-on.

In a similar sense, agoraphobia and social anxiety disorder have the same power to debilitate us through fearing a hypothetical, 'worst-case scenario' outcome. Although these anxiety disorder types may not have that many physically damaging after-effects, these anxiety types can still have the power to physically, emotionally and mentally debilitate someone at the moment. Giving power to these anxiety types also fuels the belief that you put into your negative thoughts. When you fuel these negative thoughts, you then start to create the world that you painted and perceive in your head. For instance, if you suffer from an agoraphobic fear for shopping malls, you may have false ideas in your head that shopping malls are dangerous because you can run into a mugger in the parking lot. Therefore, you refuse to go to shopping centers and try to avoid them at all costs. You may even willingly pay more to have groceries and items delivered to you, and even cancel meetings with friends at malls due to this irrational fear. What's worse is that *because* you've paid attention to the negative aspects of malls, your brain will start to look for evidence to back its theory up. For instance, you may come across a new article that states that there was a shoplifting incident at a mall near you. Your brain will latch onto these small incidents and treat them as solid reasons why malls are bad places. In doing so, your mind is literally creating a world of fear and constant anxiety. The issue with these anxiety types is that although it may seem as though the simple answer to this phobia is to reduce visits to the mall, our brain starts to normalize feelings of fear and anxiety. Once our brain finds proof that the hypotheses it comes up with are correct (for instance, finding proof that malls are bad), it will start to spiral into negative feelings such as fear and anxiety, thus giving those feelings more power and control over our lives and minds.

The effects of separation anxiety can be significant. The more that we feed into the fear that we are incapable of doing anything without our safety net (whether that's a person, a place or an object) can be extremely debilitating to our ability to grow and prosper as an individual. Separation anxiety can also greatly affect the development of our own individual identity. In addition to this, separation anxiety can trigger all the normal symptoms that come with GAD—trembling, shortness of breath, nausea, panic, hopelessness, confusion/disorientation, a feeling of being lost or helpless, etc. Separation anxiety can also trigger depression, and can also be triggered by past traumatic events. Naturally, the effects of separation anxiety aren't conducive to one's ability to grow.

As covered previously, medication-induced anxiety can trigger various physical, mental and emotional side-effects such as nausea, cold sweats, shivering/trembling, a feeling of desperation etc. Effects of this anxiety type can lead to a lack in concentration or being present at the moment and a feeling of needing the medication/drug to be able to function optimally. Understandably, the medication or substance which you are trying to wean yourself off of is something which can cause long term physical and mental health harm if the use is continued. On the opposite end of the spectrum, you will experience deprivation and withdrawal symptoms along with symptoms of anxiety. A prime example of this is the use of pain medication (morphine, for instance, can be highly addictive). While pain medication can be helpful in safe doses, the overuse of it can have damaging effects on our organs such as the liver and kidneys. Therefore, the use of it is limited to as little as possible. However, as pain killers aim to relieve the pain as much as possible, once the medication has worn off, you'll be feeling some form of pain again (but milder than when you first needed medication). This sensation can put you in a shock, as the discomfort of the pain can leave you feeling as though you need more medication to relieve the pain, thus leaving you feeling reliant on the medication. When you're reliant on the medication but can't take it anymore, that's when the anxiety aspect starts to kick in. Depending on your level of reliance on the medication/drug, the more severe the symptoms of anxiety will be. Some anxious periods can last longer than others, depending on the severity of the reliance.

NEGATIVE THINKING, ANXIETY AND ITS RELATION TO OUR HEALTH

Repetitive negative thinking (RNT) and automatic negative thinking (ANT) are two correlating factors that are powerful triggers of anxiety disorder. Negative thinking (as discussed in the previous chapter) is a way of thinking that is harmful to our growth and understanding of the world we live in. Negative thoughts can influence how we handle our relationships with others and ourselves.

RNT and ANT are negative thoughts, just in excessive amounts. They are so excessive that the thoughts turn into beliefs and can start to define our lives and the world we perceive. Once our minds have gotten used to these negative thoughts, it can easily jump to them as a definitive conclusion, before considering any other factors in the equation. This is the point when negative thoughts turn into ANTs and RNTs.

It's not only the mere fact that RNTs and ANTs can trigger anxiety disorders, it's that the combination of RNTs, ANTs and anxiety disorders have the power to create a negative snowball effect in our lives. They have the power to dictate and influence our lives to reduce our quality of living, our mental and physical health—a buildup of these factors can even lead to heightened risks of other diseases later on in life. One of the more noteworthy effects of RNTs is that it can increase your risk of dementia and Alzheimer's disease (Pratt, 2020).

Aside from the long term effects that RNTs and ANTs have on our health, these intrusive thought patterns feed off of irrational fears and worries that we have, and they have the power to push us into states of crippling anxiety. RNTs and ANTs are persistent thoughts that look for evidence to back up these intrusive thoughts and fuel our levels of anxiety, forcing us into believing and giving them the power to influence our current way of living.

The relationship and correlation between anxiety disorder, RNTs and ANTs don't only have the power to upset our current mood, but rather have the power to hinder our ability to function optimally while also increasing our risks of neurodegenerative diseases at a later point in time. In essence, the power of one's mind can truly create and define the quality of our life, the longevity of our life and our levels of physical health. Our minds can quite literally create a world of stress that can influence our physical health.

LOOKING FORWARD TO THE FIVE TECHNIQUES THAT WILL ELIMINATE NEGATIVE THINKING AND REDUCE ANXIETY

With that being said, we're now able to understand elements of our own mind that could potentially trigger our body and emotions to react in a negative way (through stress and anxiety). We have also come to understand how deeply rooted such issues could be, and how they all relate back to the core matter of how our brain processes situations. We have also come to understand how normalized we've made these negative thought processes and habits without realizing their powerful relation to other symptoms which we experience, such as anxiety and its related symptoms.

However, now that we have become more conscious of this correlation as well as the impact that it has on our quality of life, we can now move onto understanding how to better it. In the next few chapters, we will be breaking down a few powerful techniques and tools for practicing mindfulness and protecting the betterment of your mental, emotional and physical health. As we move forward in the read, it's important to practice being consciously aware of the triggers, ANTs, RNTs and anxiety symptoms that you may be experiencing, so that you can explore their root causes (the reason for their existence) and then move onto experimenting with the techniques provided to combat these intrusive thoughts and symptoms.

We will also be exploring ways of 'reprogramming' our minds. When we refer to this concept, we are simply referring to the notion of turning automatic and repetitive *negative* thoughts into automatic and repetitive *positive* thoughts. By reprogramming our minds, we will be able to identify negative and intrusive thoughts much faster, then be able to question the reality of those thoughts as well as how productive and helpful they are to our health and growth. Reprogramming our minds will also allow us to combat those negative thoughts with thoughts that uplift you and help you grow and learn —ultimately bettering our quality of life and health, as well as allowing us to function more optimally. You will also notice a change in energy levels as you release the weighty thoughts that drain your energy, and thus become more motivated and energetic.

After that, we will focus on how to practice more positive self-talk, so that if you do encounter periods of anxiousness, you can work through it with positive affirmations. We will also explore a few simple yet powerful techniques to train your mind towards becoming more positive. These techniques are all *less* than three minutes, so they're extremely quick and easy to practice regularly to promote a healthy and balanced mind, while managing to control your anxiety, stress and emotions in a healthy manner.

We will then move onto reframing your thoughts to

promote healthy thinking, as well as analyze how your judgement of a scenario has the potential to be distorted by emotions or biases. In this chapter, we will also be exploring CBT and how it can be practiced and used to combat cognitive distortions. The CBT exercises that we will be exploring are also quick and easy exercises which are all five minutes or less; therefore it can be incorporated into your regular mindfulness practice. It's important to note that although these exercises and techniques which we will be exploring are quick and simple exercises, the power that they possess lies in how often you practice them. You should be aiming to practice these mindfulness techniques about twice a day (after waking up in the morning, and before going to sleep at night), although you can determine how often you'd like to start out and work your way up from there. After all, any positive mindfulness practice is better than none at all!

Lastly, we will explore other efficient ways to keep yourself motivated while also looking at negative habits to break out of, and how to do so. The next few chapters are jam-packed with all of the tools that you need to reboot your energy and motivational levels within a month. Generally speaking, it does take a month to break old habits and adopt new ones, so you will need a bit of discipline for the first weeks of practicing mindfulness, reprogramming your thought patterns and kicking out old habits. After that, these exercises and thought processes will become much easier!

Chapter 3

First Technique to Use Affirmations to Reprogram Your Negative Self-Talk

"An affirmation can work because it has the ability to program your mind into believing the stated concept."

· Alexander, 2011

Affirmations have become increasingly popular recently and serve as an important mindfulness technique. Inspired by mantras and chants, affirmations have proven to have positive healing effects on both the conscious and subconscious mind. In addition to this, practicing daily affirmations can also help combat symptoms of anxiety and negative self-talk. It can also help balance out the absurdities and beliefs that come with cognitive distortions, while placing you in an overall better mood.

Essentially, positive affirmations are short and simple phrases that you chant repeatedly to yourself, so as to affirm confidence and belief in yourself. Considering that RNTs and ANTs cause anxiety, we can combat them by ensuring that we give attention to positive thoughts and affirmations.

These affirmative statements hold a lot of power, as they revolve around repetitive phrases that involve a specific and desired outcome or who you want to be. For instance, if you suffer from thoughts that you aren't good enough to get a job at your dream company, you can try to combat these RNTs with practicing positive affirmations such as saying "I am worthy of working in this company" or "I am skilled enough for the position I've applied for." You could even use simpler phrases such as "I am worthy," "I am skilled," "I am good at my profession," "I am hardworking," etc.

It's also important to note that although positive affirmations can be powerful in regards to creating an ideal world, it isn't a magic spell to have everything come to you without putting in the work. For instance, you can't dictate and direct external forces with positive affirmations. Positive affirmations are practiced to help us combat our own RNTs, ANTs and anxiety by enforcing more positive beliefs, thoughts and opinions to boost our emotions, motivation and quality of life. Let's say, for example, that you want to get the job that you applied for and you're struggling with anxious thoughts in relation to that job application—you could use positive affirmations like the ones we've already mentioned.

However, energy is an *extremely* important factor to note when we look at the influence that negative thoughts versus positive thoughts have on us. Negative thoughts tend to be draining and demotivating, leaving us struggling to even achieve the bare minimum. Positive thoughts, on the other hand, have the power to boost our levels of energy and motivation, while helping us believe in ourselves, our capabilities and our worth. Nourishing our minds with positive affirmations can motivate us to not only achieve the basic daily tasks at hand, but have the power to make us *want* to achieve more for ourselves, and then give us the energy to go out and achieve greater. The energy that comes with positive affirmations can be extremely attractive for others as well—it makes them want to be a part of our lives and treat us accordingly, and if not, we are able to identify what is healthy and productive for our growth and what isn't. In addition to this, positive affirmations have the power to reduce our levels of stress and anxiety in the process.

In essence, positive affirmations reprogram our mindset to a more positive and healthier one. It allows us the chance to start seeing our own worth and capabilities, while also pushing us out of our comfort zones in a healthy and safe manner by forcing us to look forward to new experiences and reap the lessons in each encounter. And, as Alexander stated, by practicing repeated positive affirmations, we allow our brain the chance to start believing in them, thus finding more positives in the world to back up these beliefs.

For instance, if you affirm yourself with the phrase that you are confident, you may start to exude more confidence. In doing so, more people could approach you to chat or socialize, or you may be asked to take on work that requires higher levels of confidence (such as public speaking). Your mind will also back up the belief of your confidence with such positive experiences and encounters so as to further affirm the fact that you are confident. This is the power of positive affirmations: it offers us the ability to literally think our way into a better state of physical, emotional and mental health.

Practicing Affirmations

One of the easiest steps to transition into practicing positive affirmations is to spot and summarize negative thoughts into simple phrases and then combat these thoughts with an opposing idea. For instance, if you struggle with confidence issues and social anxiety, try to summarize these fears into a single concept and phrase such as, "I am scared that no one will like me if I talk to them." Then, you can move onto combating that phrase with a positive affirmation such as "I am confident and enjoy making new friends." This alteration in our thought process is how positive affirmations work toward reprogramming our minds from living in fear to looking at scenarios from another angle—an angle that promotes a feeling of eagerness to learn, experience and live.

Affirmations aim to help you create and reinforce beliefs, attitudes and behaviour patterns that are productive and conducive to your growth and independence. Practicing affirmations will boost your mood, self-esteem, motivation and optimism by triggering happy emotions within you, as you visualize and embrace those beliefs. Furthermore, affirmations push you to believe that you *can* tackle more in life (especially because you have improved energy and motivational levels), so you will actively want to put in more effort into bettering yourself, solving problems, finding constructive solutions and even achieving your goals. It's such a powerful tool that it can even influence you to work towards addressing your negative thoughts from a different angle—rather than falling victim to your negative thoughts, affirmations will help you to consider exploring the negative thoughts and finding creative ways to heal from them, grow from them and empower yourself.

When we consider positive affirmations, they need to be based around core values and successes, thus triggering more positive emotions and energy to arise, such as excitement, eagerness, self-belief, etc. You can also base your affirmations around values that you want to affirm within yourself, for instance, if you value humility, you can affirm this within yourself as well as how you'd like to extend humility unto others. By identifying values that you appreciate and want to affirm within your own mind, you're allowing your mind to place conscious and subconscious focus on those positive values, thus promoting greater self-empowerment.

Now that we understand how to properly make use of them without expectations placed on them, we need to then move onto how often one must practice these exercises. As with anything in life, the full effect of affirmations can only be felt when it's practiced often. Because affirmations have the potential to be so powerful and life-altering, they need to be practiced often, as if you were trying to take on a new habit. Considering that we've made RNTs and ANTs a habit, we need to make positive affirmations a habit to combat and eliminate the habit of negative thinking.

The first step which you will need to take to create a habit out of practicing affirmations is to practice the affirmations everyday for 30 days, for 2-5 minutes in the morning and 2-5 minutes in the evening (Klein, 2020). Try to repeat each affirmation 10 times each, so that it can sink in and allow you to feel comfortable with the phrase. For instance, saying "I am confident" ten times to yourself has much more impact and forces you to believe in it, as opposed to simply stating it once.

You should also aim to keep the affirmations relevant to your current life situation and thought processes. Affirmations need to constantly be revisited and restructured in accordance with what you're currently going through.

You can also try to make the process easier by keeping affirmation notes around your home or workplace, wherever you will see them often. Keeping little post-it notes on your wall or even typing affirmations into your phone/laptop to keep on hand can help reinforce the affirmations. If you journal, you could also try to write them in the front of your journal and go over them twice a day before journaling.

Positive affirmations aren't required to be practiced twice a day. This is just a general guideline to help start and end your days in a positive mood, allow you to reflect on the day and realign and process your thoughts and emotions. You should also aim to practice reciting positive affirmations when you encounter negative thoughts or anxiety throughout the day, rather than entertain them. Try to spot trigger thoughts, scenarios or words that lead to negative thoughts or anxiety, and when you notice these factors start to trigger you, immediately combat them with positive affirmations. A prime example of this can be to substitute your "I can't" excuses with "I don't." This can already remove so much power from the negative thoughts that fuel your anxiety. By believing in the phrase that you 'can't' do something, you're placing a limit on yourself for absolutely no solid reason other than you simply not wanting to do something. So, instead, try to substitute that "I can't" excuse with an "I don't want to," so that you still have the option to do something and you know that you have the ability to do it.

It's also important to note that positive affirmations aren't going to completely eradicate anxiety and negative thoughts—they're part of our human nature! You aren't going to turn into a "yes man" once you start practicing positive affirmations; you will still have the ability to choose what you want to do with your life and how you want to live your life, but by practicing positive affirmations, you have the ability to regain the power to make those decisions.

Lastly, if you're comfortable enough to do so, consider mentioning this exercise to your close friends and family who you often talk to or confide in. They can also be able to help you through this process and bring your attention to negative thought patterns (Steber, 2016). Sometimes it's difficult for us to pinpoint our own habits on our own, so having a second pair of eyes or ears on the matter can greatly speed up the process. If you are considering confiding in someone, it's important that you trust them wholeheartedly as some people have the potential to take advantage of this situation and gaslight you, making the healing process much more tedious, confusing and emotionally exhausting.

AFFIRMATIONS IN FIVE EASY STEPS

Creating your set of affirmations can be done in a simple, five-step process. Naturally, these affirmations can be adjusted as you go through life.

The first step is to identify what your current RNTs, ANTs and anxiety triggers are. This will require a level of self-awareness, so take as much time as you need to assess your negative thoughts or thoughts that may be limiting you from living your life optimally (Alexander, 2011). Try to identify with any thoughts that you feel are triggering your anxiety or even thoughts that simply drain your energy. For instance, if you wake up in the morning and instantly have thoughts along the lines of "I don't want to wake up right now," "I want to stay in bed," "I don't want to exercise," "I don't want to go to work today" or any other thoughts that act as excuses, drain your energy and leave you feeling demotivated. All of these thoughts can be easily combated with thoughts along the line of "I'm thankful for my job," "I can't wait to feel good after this morning workout," "If I get up now, I'll be able to relax and take my time eating my breakfast before work." Simple thought alterations such as these can also fall under positive affirmations to fuel your mind with motivation and positive energy.

Next, you will need to create and write down positive affirmation phrases which combat those negative thoughts, or simply write down positive phrases which will help you become the person that you want to be. For instance, writing down values that you wish to uphold, such as "I am grateful," or "I am worthy." You can also ask your close friends and family for qualities that they admire about you, to help instill these values within yourself.

After this, you should work on practicing these affirmations daily. This is where the above section comes into play—creating a habit out of practicing the affirmations and repeating the phrases so that they can sink in. As mentioned before, you will need to say the repeated affirmations out loud to yourself every morning and evening (at least), and you can then also repeat these affirmations to yourself throughout the day if need be. In addition to this, you should aim to say each phrase/affirmation at least ten times to feel the full effect of it. You can, however, repeat the phrase/affirmation a specific number of times if you have a lucky number or special number. For instance, if you believe in angel numbers and have a lucky number (for instance, say that this number is 'seven'), then you can repeat each affirmation seven times. You should also aim to stand in front of a mirror and say the affirmations out loud, while looking at yourself (so as to treat your reflection as a friend that you were telling these affirmations to).

The fourth step focuses on anchoring the affirmation within your body and mind. This is done by practicing breath work while also taking note of any areas in your body that feel stressed or uneasy at the anxiety caused by RNTs and ANTs. A prime example of this is that when we feel stressed out, we may experience stomach cramps or tightness in the chest. When practicing your positive affirmations, aim to take deep breaths as you say each phrase out loud, while placing your hand over the area that reacts to the negative thoughts. In doing so, you're in a sense 'healing' the stress that those body areas go through, when dealing with negative thoughts or experiences.

The final point is to get a trusted friend, family member or coach to repeat the affirmations back to you. Often we can feel comfortable talking to ourselves and even complimenting ourselves, but when someone else does it, we can sometimes have a hard time accepting the compliment. If however, you aren't too comfortable with asking someone else to reinforce affirmations with you, you can work with the mirror and treat your reflection as a friend!

If you are truly struggling to identify your negative thoughts or find positive affirmations that combat those negative thoughts, you can seek professional help from a therapist to help you identify the thoughts or triggers. Alternatively, practicing mindful meditation can also help you tap into your subconscious and identify what your anxious thoughts are. When practicing mindfulness and meditation, you're essentially aiming to accept the reality of the situations you face so as to raise your levels of self-awareness. In doing so, it allows change and healing to happen. Practicing mindfulness can be in the form of meditation, journaling or doing something that's healthily cathartic, such as exercising, dancing, hiking, swimming, painting, etc.

To summarize, the five steps for affirmations can be categorized as:

1. Identifying negative thoughts/habits.
2. Combat those thoughts by writing down positive affirmations.
3. Repeat the affirmations out-loud for at least five minutes in the morning and the evening.
4. Work on anchoring those affirmations within your body.
5. Find others to repeat who are willing to repeat the affirmations back to you, or repeat them in front of your mirror.

THE STARTING POINT AND CREATING YOUR OWN SET OF AFFIRMATIONS

To expand on the second point, it is one of the toughest to tackle, as well as one of the most powerful points. This is due to the fact that these are the new thoughts and perceptions which you're training your mind to believe in. The best way to start with positive affirmations is to keep them as simple as possible.

When you identify negative thoughts, RNTs, ANTs, or triggers for anxiety, you should try to summarize these concepts in their most absolute and basic form. If, for instance, you struggle with relationships because of past trauma, try to identify one key element or word that your anxiety and negative thoughts feed off of. Let's say that in this case, you're afraid of the relationship ending badly. You will need to combat these fears with thoughts of how deserving you are of good and healthy relationships, and that these relationships won't define your worth, but serve to teach you valuable lessons. This can be summarized down to "I deserve love," or "I am worthy," or even "I am lovable."

The best and most efficient way to tackle affirmations is to summarize them in impactful words that are valuable to you. For instance, "I am worthy" stems from the word 'worth.' This simple yet powerful word can work to combat so many doubts and anxiety symptoms.

A few other important points to consider when determining and creating your own affirmations is to begin your affirmations with 'I' or 'my' so that you're starting your phrase off strongly and instilling power in it. By starting with either 'I' or 'my', you're instilling the idea that you already possess those qualities within yourself—it's just a matter of believing in them, and in turn, believing in yourself. It's also important to note that because the words with which you've chosen to combat the negative thoughts are personal and specific to you, it adds much more power to the phrase by adding in the possession of 'I' or 'my.'

Aim to keep the phrases current so that you're also not procrastinating on your own growth. For instance, don't say "I'll be confident once I finish my public speaking course," or "I'll prove my worth once I prove my point in this meeting." Rather, aim to possess those qualities at the moment (within the affirmations) so that you create the space, energy and attitude necessary to see those situations through. For instance, it shouldn't take a situation, encounter or experience to prove these basic values to you. You need to hone in on them so that whether the situation goes well or badly, it doesn't affect you, how you continue to carry yourself.

It's also important to note that you shouldn't aim to block out any anxious thoughts that you may encounter, even while practicing positive affirmations. Rather, try to question and explore them so that you can adjust your affirmations accordingly. Don't try to disown anxiety within your affirmations either. For example, rather than saying "my anxiety won't affect my life any longer," try to reword the phrase to say "I can achieve anything, despite my anxiety." In doing so, you're being realistic about the fact that anxiety does exist and that millions experience it, rather than blocking it out and not acknowledging that it's a factor which many of us face. If you do disregard these emotions, you may create a negative perception of what 'anxiety' is, rather than embracing it and working with it; therefore, it's extremely important to consider how you can work with it to still achieve all of your goals.

For the most powerful affirmations, aim for the affirmation to be: in the present tense, positive, and concise. Your affirmative words need to include action, emotion and value. Action affirmations promote motivation towards achieving physical goals, for instance, visualising yourself succeeding in something specific and experiencing that moment. Action affirmations promote the Law of Attraction as you motivate yourself towards achieving something. An example of this would be "I can achieve so many more work goals now that I have my degree." Athletes tend to practice this form of affirmation prior to playing their sports matches, and they visualize themselves achieving their goals for the match. In doing so, they're getting in the headspace to achieve those goals while also helping them focus on the specific goal.

Adding emotion into the affirmation can also help you get into the feelings that come with achieving something. Emotion and value affirmations go hand-in-hand with one another to help anchor the feelings that come with the affirmation. An example of this would be, "I am grateful for the new job opportunities that are going to come my way with my degree."

There are a plethora of positive words that you can fill into your daily affirmations, but here are a few examples to prompt you ("Daily Affirmations for Positive Thinking," n.d.):

- Bold
- Appreciated
- Humble

- Happy
- Inspired
- Strong
- Valuable/Valued
- Warm
- Free
- Extraordinary
- Worthy
- Proud
- Powerful
- Grateful
- Fun
- Confident
- Trusting
- Approachable
- Passionate
- Eager

Lastly, affirmations should not come with expectations, they should be repeated and then released. For instance, if your affirmation is that you're proud to be getting so many job opportunities coming your way, then you need to trust that it will come to you, without expecting it to come. Remember that affirmations exist for you to reprogram your brain, emotions and attitude to a more positive setting and look at every experience as a lesson, without expecting anything. With expectations comes the risk of disappointment, which has the power to trigger you back into a negative pattern of thinking and victimization. Aim to keep your affirmations positive, clear, and remember to anchor them so that you familiarize your mind and body with positive feelings, thoughts and energy!

Chapter 4

Second Technique to Positively Train Your Brain Using Three-Minute Methods

"NLP is used as a method of personal development through promoting skills, such as self-reflection, confidence, and communication."

· Kandola, 2017

As we work through methods to efficiently reprogram our minds toward more positive and constructive thoughts, the neuro-linguistic programming

(NLP) methods are certainly a method worth mentioning.

The NLP methods have been practiced since the 1970s. The idea of NLP was originated by Richard Bandler and John Grinder, who aimed at studying and identifying patterns of thoughts and behaviours of successful people, so as to assist others in working towards training their own minds in a similar method.

There are a few methods and patterns with which NLP works—one of the most popular methods is the NLP Swish method (which we will be exploring within this chapter). The NLP methods were mostly used to treat symptoms of phobias and anxiety, thus promoting greater performance levels and an overall higher quality of life (Kandola, 2017). NLP works to alter one's thoughts, behaviour, attitude and levels of motivation to assist them in achieving their goals and desired outcomes. In doing so, NLP aims its focus towards identifying negative thought patterns and helping evolve those thoughts into positive, constructive thoughts.

Through the practice of NLP methods, you will see results in greater self-awareness, greater control of your emotions, levels of energy and motivation, and an overall higher quality of life. Heightened levels of self-awareness can reduce levels of anxiety, stress and worry by training our minds to look at situations from all angles and not only the negative aspects (which can trigger higher levels of fear and anxiety, as well as cause your mind to hypothesize worst-case scenarios to brood over).

How Does NLP Work?

The study of NLP is based around the idea that humans work with internal, mental 'maps' of the world, and that our minds create these maps to connect the dots of all of our experiences and encounters, in an attempt to better understand the world with less energy exhausted in the process. The issue with these mental 'maps' is that our minds can often reach further by hypothesizing outcomes from familiar experiences, factors and triggers. These hypotheses can also be influenced by our emotions—thus resulting in fears and triggers for anxiety.

This is precisely what NLP aims to cover—working through these mental maps via conscious conversations to identify one's thought patterns and behaviours. Preferred representational system (PRS) is a tool that is critical to NLP. Essentially, PRS is used to identify and create methods to reprogram the mind by first identifying what senses we are biased towards. For instance, when someone says "I see your point," they are triggering a visual PRS.

Once these sensory biases are determined, we can then use that PRS to further explore our thought frameworks and adjust them accordingly. These thought frameworks (for reprogramming our minds through NLP) can consist of information gathering, rapport building and goal setting. Information gathering will help us understand the root causes or triggers of the negative thoughts; rapport building will cover understanding our behaviour, attitude and energy through different techniques and exercises; and goal-setting will naturally assist us in creating and achieving goals.

A few of the methods that NLP makes use of are: anchoring, rapport, swish pattern and visual/kinesthetic dissociation (VKD). Anchoring is when we identify specific sensory experiences which trigger different emotions, and vice versa, thus allowing us to gain better control over our emotions. It aims to understand where we hold tension for that specific emotion, and then work with that area or sensory experience to exercise our responses to situations. Anchoring can come in the form of a word, gesture or even an image (Margues, n.d.). When practicing anchoring, you will need to identify a specific scenario where you experienced intense positive feelings, such as a proud achievement. Consider the senses that were triggered during this scenario. What did you see, feel, or hear? Next, bring these intense positive feelings towards a specific sense in your body (known as a sensory cue). This could be lightly squeezing one of your fingers, pinching your earlobe, or wherever you would like to anchor this feeling. After a few minutes, take a break and then repeat the process until you've associated a specific sensory cue with that positive feeling. Now, whenever you need to access a quick release of positive feelings (especially when placed in a stressful situation or environment) you can easily turn to your sensory cue to release those positively affiliated emotions.

The rapport method is done by having a practitioner or professional match your emotional responses and physical behaviour to assist you in identifying your triggers as well as improving communicative skills and response to empathy.

The swish pattern is the method which we will be covering later on in this chapter. It's one of the most commonly used methods and can be practiced with others or on its own. It's a method that changes our thought and behavioral patterns in an attempt to reprogram our minds to handle scenarios with more constructive outlooks. It's a simple yet powerful technique to direct attention to our responses, and adjust them to be more efficient and productive.

The last method mentioned, the VKD method, aims to remove negative thoughts and feelings that are associated with situations from the past. This can help those that suffer from PTSD or have biases based on passed events, and need to heal from these events. In doing so, those that work with the VKD method can heal from past events as well as realign their thoughts, responses and behaviour to be more conducive for current and future events.

NLP SWISH PATTERN

The NLP Swish technique is essentially an effi-

cient way of identifying negative thoughts and anxieties which you may be possessing or dealing with.
The method then assists you in eliminating your negative thoughts, emotions and biases so that you can
swap these factors with more positive emotions and
thoughts to promote healthy healing, growth and
learning. In doing so, it reduces your levels of anxiety.

One of the most popular ways to practice the NLP
Swish method is by detaching yourself from the
memory or thought, then determining how you would
like to handle the situation and feel, and then combining those two elements together. Afterwards, you
will practice visualizing yourself dealing with that
memory or thought with how you'd like to handle
the situation, until those thought processes and emotions are habitual in the triggering experience. The
first phase of this exercise can be considered the 'set
up' phase, where you work towards identifying the
negative thoughts, triggers and emotions, while also
identifying the reality of the situation as well as how
you would like to feel toward the situation that you're
in (Wiley, n.d.). The second step in the NLP Swish
method is understood as the 'replacement' phase.
This step aims to start anchoring those positive
thoughts within you, while visualizing handling the
triggers which tend to upset you. Try to remain in
control when you are visualizing the situation. As you
continue practicing and become more comfortable
with the process, you can immerse yourself further
into gaining control over your emotions and thoughts,

so that you aren't overwhelmed by the experience. Now, I'll offer a quick explainer of both phases.

1. The Set-Up:

· Identify the unwanted emotions in the situation that you're in. A great way of identifying these could be to determine whether or not these emotions or thoughts help the situation in any way. Aim to answer: are these emotions and thoughts helping you solve problems, or are they fueling your need to brood over the situation? Are these emotions making you doubt your capabilities? Are these emotions and thoughts giving you energy to achieve your desired outcomes or are they draining you of your energy? All of those unwanted emotions and thoughts need to be identified so that they can be changed.

· Spot your triggers: Aim to try and identify all of the factors that could be triggering your negative thoughts, emotions and reactions. These triggers can come in any form—from a simple phrase or word that someone says to you, to an event or encounter which you have to face. Triggers can even come in the form of foods. For instance, if you eat too much fast food, you may feel sluggish, lethargic, depressed and unmotivated. Try to experiment with different aspects of your lifestyle, from conversations, to places, to your diet to see which factors trigger negative emotions or thoughts for you. You will have to be extremely aware when identifying your triggers, because some triggers can be extremely discrete and sneaky in the way in which they set-off your emotions. Most triggers affect our subconscious, so it's difficult to then try to consciously spot them. You can analyze your emotions, thoughts and even symptoms of anxiety as tools to help spot where the triggers are coming from. For instance, if you notice that you get agitated at family get-togethers, try to pay closer attention in these scenarios to see exactly what is triggering you from those situations. It could be that you don't like your family's way of communicating with one another, or that they place pressure on you by interrogating your personal life. These are a few examples of ways to spot specific triggers.

· Fact checks your situation: Often, our perception of reality can be misconstrued by our own emotions, biases, experiences and fears. We can combat the power which these negative emotions and fears have on our perception of a situation by simply fact checking the validity of these emotions. For instance, if you have negative thoughts, fears or biases regarding driving, you can always fact check the validity of those fears by seeing how safe the roads truly are. The point aims to put your fears and negative thoughts in perspective, rather than letting those negative thoughts and fears completely influence you.

· Consider how you'd like to feel: This last factor is so vitally important to consider, as it offers you a 'goal' throughout the whole process. Once you've identified what you'd like to change, that's already a major improvement in heightening your level of self-awareness. However, this last step allows us to identify, visualize and work towards the change that we want to achieve. When identifying how you'd like to feel, you will need to consider all of the above factors as well. For instance, consider how you'd like to react to your triggers or how you'd like to think when fact-checking triggering situations. Once you have identified how you'd like to feel, you can then move onto visualizing that feeling, especially when faced with a triggering situation. By visualizing your ideal, desired emotions toward those triggering situations, you can gain a sense of self-empowerment while also allowing yourself to see that there are ways to positively handle that situation.

1. The Replacement:

· Start by visualizing the trigger that upsets you. If there are words or sounds that trigger you, visualize its source. If you're triggered by criticism in regards to your work, try to visualize your boss or a client critiquing your work.

· Then, step out of the situation and imagine as though you were watching the scenario play out on a TV screen.

· Replace the old version of how you would handle the situation with a newer version of how you want to handle it. Visualize yourself absorbing the situation, imagine how your thought processes would work at the moment, and then visualize how you'd like to react to that scenario. In doing so, ensure that this visualization leaves you feeling empowered at the end. If we take the simple example of watching any movie or TV series, we always root for the protagonist to end up overcoming their obstacles and prevailing at the end of the show. Similarly, you need to visualize yourself as the protagonist in your own challenging situation, but imagine yourself prevailing and overcoming your obstacle.

· Take a mental break from the scenario and bring yourself back to the present moment. Allow your mind and emotions to realign with the current time and try to remove yourself emotionally and mentally from the exercise by doing something to distract yourself—this could be watching an episode or reading a few pages in a book. Once you feel calmer and ready to tackle the exercise again, you can repeat this step. You will need to repeat this step a few times (about

5-7 times), but try to speed up the visualization process each time, as well as speeding up your ability to react to the situation (in the manner which you'd like to react).

1. Once you feel as though you have familiarized yourself well enough with how you would like to react to the triggering event, you will then need to test it to see if you have instilled faster and more productive responses and emotions within yourself. In this step, you will need to go back to a triggering memory or triggering hypothetical scenario, and place yourself at that moment (this time, you are at the moment and not watching it play out on a screen).

When recalling the memory or experiencing the hypothetical scenario, your aim is to not have any negative thoughts, stresses or anxiety from the situation. If the scenario does trigger negative thoughts or emotions, then you will need to go through step two a few more times, until the negative thoughts and emotions have gone.

It's also important that when working through the Swish process that you relax as you move through the process—especially because you're going to be working through some triggering experiences, thoughts and emotions. We cannot force ourselves to heal. It takes time and practice of facing our triggers authentically and head-on. Take as much time and practice as you need, otherwise the healing process may be ineffective.

Overall, the NLP Swish method aims to target and reduce the amount of negative thoughts which we may experience in a triggering scenario by simply becoming aware of the alternative options for reactions towards a situation. It aims to challenge our own minds to question desirable outcomes within those situations and then start to visualize them, and in turn, train our minds to believe that alternative reactions are possible and that we can empower ourselves in triggering scenarios.

USING NLP TO COMBAT RNTS AND ANXIETY

Research studies uncovered that our brains cannot tell the difference between real and visualized experiences as they both use the same parts of our brain ("These 4 NLP Techniques Could Change How You Think," n.d.). Similarly, we can relate this back to when we use our negative emotions to fuel fears, phobias and "worst-case scenario" outcomes. Our brain has the power to hypothesize terrible outcomes. In turn, this can lead to us experiencing crippling anxiety, and an overall fear for those outcomes (whether they are realistic or not). However, NLP aims to combat this by training our minds to also see that there are ways to visualize positive outcomes, just as much as we entertain the negative ones.

In addition to this, NLP Swish also promotes better cognitive skills, greater memory, attention and perception, as well as a greater ability to control your emotions and reactions! The NLP Swish also trains you to approach situations in a much calmer and more confident manner, while remaining highly self-aware. In doing so, not only are the effects of anxiety reduced, but our risk of long term mental health issues are reduced.

It's also important to note within this section that the NLP Swish method can actually promote higher levels of anxiety if not done correctly. If, for example, you create an unrealistic ideal version of yourself to handle triggering situations and you can't meet that expectation in reality, it will leave you feeling more confused and stressed than before. For instance, if you are working through a triggering memory of arguing with your narcissistic boss who threatens your job if you stand up to them, and you visualize yourself challenging them and eventually becoming the boss of the company. This could be a considerably unrealistic scenario. What's worse is that you visualize this fantasy scenario so much that you create a new distorted script in your head of how you want to handle the situations. When you're faced with the situation and it doesn't go according to how you'd planned, it will naturally cause you to go back into a panic.

This aspect of NLP can cover what we consider 'meta-modelling'. Meta-modelling is another method within NLP that works on either end of the thought and emotive spectrum: It can help to pinpoint negative thoughts and emotions, or positive thoughts and emotions. This method can also help us spot how realistic our NLP Swish responses are.

The meta-modelling method mainly covers the idea that we place expectations or hypothetical biases on factors, limiting ourselves from seeing the overall picture. Meta-modeling is broken down into three key aspects:

- **Generalizing**: this is where we take parts of a thought, experience, encounter or factor and make a general bias over it. For example, thinking that all of your relationships will end badly.
- **Distortions**: this covers the aforementioned idea that we aren't being realistic with our perception or visualization of a scenario. We are only focusing on specific areas and placing expectations on other factors to react accordingly. We need to also be careful about scripting our visualizations, because this can also be considered placing an expectation on an event or encounter.
- **Deletions**: this covers the notion that our minds pick and choose specific sections of a scenario so as to aid a pre-existing belief (or fear, in this case). For instance, if we are receiving feedback or critique on work, our minds could filter out the positive criticism and only focus on the areas that need to be worked upon. In doing so, this can fuel our anxiety and enhance the believability of pre-existing fears and worries.

HOW TO MAKE THE NLP SWISH PATTERN WORKS
FOR YOU

In understanding the above three categories for meta-modeling, we can then assess how realistic our NLP Swish responses are. Aim to consider whether the responses which you have created towards the triggering memory or thought limits you in any way, distorts the reality of the situation in any way, places any expectations on factors within the scenario, or hyper-focuses on specific areas of the triggering memory.

The aim of NLP and reprogramming is to authentically heal and reprogram our minds to have more efficient responses to scenarios, responses that aren't biased or unrealistic in any way. Healing and positive affirmations cannot take place unless there is authenticity in the healing and reprogramming phases.

You can also use the three categories highlighted in meta-modelling to see if you may be distorting, generalising or deleting factors of situations which trigger you. Afterwards, you can use the Swish method to work through these triggering situations. Essentially, we can make use of the Swish method and the meta-modeling method together or treat them as separate methods.

When assessing the impact of your practice of any of the NLP methods, you should aim to test how quickly you respond to the triggering situation (even if it's just through a visualization). You should aim to fill your mind with positive and constructive thoughts that assist you in logically processing all factors of the triggering situation, and then note how you respond emotionally, verbally and physically to the situation. At the end of the day, we need to try to completely reframe our thought processes so that we are embodying the person that we visualized (in step two of the Swish method). We need to fully embrace the thoughts, emotions and senses of who we want to be when placed in triggering situations. If you're still feeling hesitant, anxious or are experiencing subtle hints of negative thoughts arising, you need to continue the visualization practice until you're able to fully embrace the change.

Chapter 5

Third Technique to Reframe Your Thoughts Under 5 Minutes

The power of a positive mind doesn't merely allow us to simply *feel* happier, it also raises our levels of energy and motivation. Most importantly, positive thinking allows us to create a calm and supportive space within our minds to find solutions towards the problems which we face, or are triggered by.

However, positive thinking isn't only a solution for short-term relief. It also has the power to physically change the way our body copes and reacts to the situations that trigger us. Symptoms of anxiety can be greatly reduced or even eliminated by the simple yet powerful reframing of our thought patterns. What has been most astounding, is the discovery of the linkage from our mental habits to diseases in old age—such as neurodegenerative diseases, diabetes and even heart disease. It's commonly known that high levels of stress are interlinked with higher risks of cardiovascular disease, but studies have delved much deeper than that in the recent years.

Additionally, regularly practicing mindfulness exercises has been proven to strengthen the prefrontal cortex of our brain; thus promoting a more optimal functioning of cognitive skills, a longer memory and attention span, an overall heightened level of awareness and greater controllability of one's emotions. Mindful practices come in many forms, some of the most obvious ways being practicing meditation, yoga and journaling. However, exercises that tackle NLP and cognitive behavioural therapy can also fall under this category, but help us identify, target and work through more of the deep-rooted thought habits which we possess.

The remainder of this chapter will be dedicated to providing more insight into cognitive behavioral therapy, specifically explaining how you can utilize it at home (with an exercise that takes less than 5 minutes!) in order to reduce your anxiety and improve your overall quality of life.

An Insight into Cognitive Distortions

Cognitive behavioral therapy (also known as CBT) is essentially a form of therapy to assist us in thinking in a more positive, healthy and productive manner. If we can quickly relate this back to the previous chapter, we had emphasized the idea that although we can determine and visualize how we would *like* to handle a situation, we still need that reaction to be a realistic and rational one in relation to the given scenario. With CBT, we aim to work through how to determine how to realistically and rationally identify appropriate thoughts and responses for the triggering situation.

Cognitive distortions, on the other hand, are what CBT aims to tackle: the idea that our minds have the tendency to distort reality based on our own beliefs. Cognitive distortions were briefly discussed in the previous chapter when we were dissecting the method of meta-modeling: the three categories of deletion, generalization and distortion.

Cognitive distortions, in their essence, are how people perceive an inaccurate version of reality, usually in a negative way. For instance, thinking that you're going to get promoted in your workplace when you haven't had enough experience working with the company. This triggers negative emotions due to the distorted reality of the scenario. You may even be further triggered by this to think that your worth isn't being recognized in the company or that you aren't good enough for the company, and then start to fear that your job might be on the line. These are all distortions that are combined with deletions (picking specific aspects of a scenario) and generalizations (thinking that you aren't good enough) to create reasoning within a distorted perception of reality.

The issue with cognitive distortions is that they're habitual, and the more that you entertain them, the more your mind looks for ways to back these distortions up and create a false sense of reality. In doing so, you start to lose motivation and energy, while living in a constant state of worry. Cognitive distortions can and do work hand-in-hand with negative thinking, as it can be considered a factor that falls under negative thinking and can trigger more negative thinking to occur.

Cognitive distortions can be completely overwhelming and leave us feeling crippled with fear and anxiety. Although cognitive distortions can be a very real factor that we all face (especially due to our fluctuations in emotions), the more crippling forms of cognitive distortions stem from negative life experiences or, in other words, traumatic experiences. The more prolonged exposure to those experiences can influence the severity and amount of cognitive distortions created to cope with such experiences. Theories have also revolved around the idea that cognitive distortions developed as an evolutionary survival method so as to help one overcome their current predicaments.

Whether these cognitive distortions were created from PTSD triggers or as a tool to mentally and emotionally get through a traumatic period, cognitive distortions aren't conducive to our growth once we've overcome those periods. Although our brain may have used these distortions as a means of coping or even surviving through a period, these habits need to be readjusted in order to heal and move forward in a healthy, less stressful manner.

As we briefly covered, a few of psychiatrist Aaron Beck's types of negative thinking fall into similar categories for types of cognitive distortions (Stanborough, 2019):

1. **Polarized thinking**: this type of thinking suggests that we only see things on either end of the spectrum without considering the factors in between (also understood as the grey area). This can cause us such stress as it can prevent us from seeing that there are multiple ways to achieve our goals. It can limit our ability to take and tackle constructive criticism which can hinder our ability to grow, manage relationships and even achieve our goals. As cheesy as it may sound, life is all about compromises and the notion that comes with polarized thinking promotes the exact opposite of that.

2. **Overgeneralization/Generalization**: when we make an overall assumption about a situation or experience that's based on deletion or labelling. In doing so, our minds are only focusing on factors that back up that generalization. For instance, if you once had a bad experience of food poisoning at a restaurant, you may want to never revisit that restaurant again, thinking that their

food makes you sick. When in reality, it may have just been one isolated bad experience.

3. **Catastrophizing**: when one believes in the worst possible outcome. If you experience the distortion of catastrophizing, you may experience your mind quickly jumping from an ordinary situation to the worst possible outcome very quickly. For instance, if you need to fly somewhere, your mind may fill up with worries about the possibility of the plane crashing. Catastrophizing can also be understood as a thread of overreactions, for instance, if you haven't received feedback on a work submission, you worry that your client may not have liked your work. This could then lead to your company losing the client, thus compromising your job with the company.

4. **Personalization**: pertains to the idea that everything that happens in life needs to be taken personally. This happens to many of us, but the problem starts when we aren't aware that we are taking things personally and then start to question ourselves, rather than considering alternate reasons for a situation playing out the way that it did. Personalization can also trigger high levels of anxiety and depression while also making us question our own self-worth and identity.

5. **Mind reading**: relates to when we try to provide reasoning for others, or determining other peoples' opinions without solid evidence to back

it up. For instance, assuming someone doesn't like you because they were quiet when they met you. While in reality, they may have just been quiet because they were having a bad day or struggle to communicate to people that they just met.

6. **Mental filtering**: the tendency to only focus (or hyper-focus) on the negative aspects to back a negative belief. This can also be understood as 'deletions', whereby our minds tend to only focus on certain parts of a scenario so as to back up its own negative thoughts/beliefs. Mental filtering is also associated with how we perceive ourselves, and it's known to worsen symptoms of depression due to increasing the feeling of hopelessness in a situation. Mental filtering is an extremely overpowering distortion to possess, especially if you're unaware of it, it's traits, characteristics and power over one's mind.

7. **Discounting the positive factors**: this aspect can go hand-in-hand with either catastrophizing and/or mental filtering. As its name suggests, discounting the positive factors essentially means that we're hyper-focusing on the negative attributes of a scenario, and placing more importance on them to the point that we can only view that given scenario with a negative approach. A prime example of this is how we tend to view ourselves. It's often said that we can sometimes be our biggest critique. This saying

can apply to the idea that we discount our own positive factors and only view ourselves in negative lights, thus limiting our confidence in our own capabilities.

8. **'Should' or 'ought to' statements**: these sort of statements and thoughts of what one 'should' be doing, thinking or behaving like, and these internalized thoughts generally stem from cultural, traditional, societal and family expectations of how situations should be handled. These 'should' statements can often limit us to explore how we would like to handle a situation on our own, and thus resulting in heightened levels of anxiety.

9. **Emotional reasoning**: pertains to the belief that all of your emotions are true and unbiased. It's important to note that emotions can greatly influence how we *perceive* reality and can often trick our minds into believing that that perception is the true reality. While emotions are greatly important to experience and shouldn't be invalidated, making judgements on situations should also consist of factual and rational based evidence. Have you found yourself reacting to and creating biases over triggering situations? This is a form of emotional reasoning. Rather than investigating the situation further, we judge an entire situation and create a response that purely stems from our emotions. Though this is a completely natural and human re-

sponse, it can sometimes hinder our ability to learn and grow from situations. Emotional reasoning can also limit us from turning negative situations into positive ones, as we respond through emotions before looking at the situation rationally.

10. **Labelling**: this is a term that can go hand-in-hand with overgeneralization. As the term suggests it involves generalising complex situations into one negative term. In doing so, we limit ourselves from giving situations, people or ourselves the benefit of the doubt.

The above ten examples are a few of the most common forms of cognitive distortions, and, as we can now see, they are similar to negative thought types. Although cognitive distortions can be extremely hard to spot and embed themselves deep in our subconscious, the good news is that now that we are able to identify them and give them names, we're also able to identify whether we possess some of these mental patterns or not. We can also explore practices and exercises to rework our thought patterns away from these distortions.

Identifying these distortions can be through various practices such as raising your levels of awareness when placed in triggering situations, or identifying these distortions through verbal communication with others, or simply through mindfulness practices such as mediation, journaling and yoga.

You can also do a cost-benefit analysis on these distortions to see how often you use them or how badly they're limiting your perception of reality. In the cost-benefit analysis, simply jot down what your cognitive distortions are and then take notes of how often they appear within the week, as well as how they limit you from going about the scenario. At the end of the week, tally up each distortion to see how heavily it affects your mental and emotional state as well as your energy levels. Ask whether you're benefiting from these thoughts or losing energy on them. If you aren't benefitting from these thoughts in any way and they're limiting you, you will then need to try a few exercises to reframe your thoughts. One of the more commonly used exercises is CBT exercises, whereby talk therapy is used to help you identify, interrupt and change unhealthy thoughts (such as cognitive distortions).

Five-Minute CBT Exercises

As mentioned in the previous section, one of the major effects of cognitive disorder and negative thinking is its hindrance of our ability to clearly perceive reality as factual, rational and logical. Distortions and negative thoughts often work hand-in-hand with draining emotions and feed off of each other to create their own reality which creates a breeding ground for even higher levels of anxiety, depression and overall lower quality of life.

Due to these thoughts being so embedded in our subconscious, we need to practice regular mindful techniques and exercises to help bring them to the surface so that they are identifiable and can then be reworked and substituted with more positive methods of dealing with reality (especially when it comes to more triggering situations).

If you would prefer a more structured and logical approach towards reframing your thoughts, the five-minute triple column technique can be of aid (Aswell, 2020). This technique can help you to physically jot down your thoughts and then examine them. The method can also help one detach from their own thoughts by first releasing all of their thoughts on a sheet and then objectively analysing and assessing those thoughts. In doing so, one can remove the emotional attachments or triggers that may prevail when working through thought patterns internally.

The five-minute triple column technique is broken down into four simple steps:

1. On a sheet of paper (or in Excel spreadsheet) create three columns.
2. Label the first column "automatic thoughts," the second column 'distortions' and the third column "rational response."
3. In the first column, you will write down any thoughts that you are experiencing which feel negative, weighty or distorted. An example of this could be that you are worried that your boss

hasn't approved of your submission yet and now you fear that you're not good enough for the company. In the second column, try to identify which cognitive distortion types are in the thoughts in the first column. For instance, this example would trigger cognitive distortions of overgeneralization, mind reading, discounting the positive factors and mental filtering. In the third column, think about opposing factors to each of those distortions so as to level out the negative elements within the distortions, and then write down a logical and rational thought in the third column. The third column should essentially counteract the first column with a more rational approach to the situation.

4. Read over or rewrite these thoughts as many times as you feel necessary, until the more rational approach (the third column) settles in your mind and eases the negative cognitive distortions.

If we had to break these scenarios up into categories specific to life scenarios, we can look at aspects such as work, finances, relationships, and parenting/family-related issues that all influence. By using the five-minute triple column method, we can easily break down any issues which we may feel stressed about and logically work through them in this exercise.

For work-related stresses, we can consider how we

process criticism as well as assess our own work ethic through the triple column method. One of the most common issues is finding a way to separate work from their personal identity. For instance, if you receive negative feedback from a client, you might find yourself brooding over their criticism all day. It could lead to you questioning your own capabilities and you could find yourself cognitively distorting the scenario. Your passion for your job may even take a hit. If you turn to the five minutes triple column technique, you can write down the criticism or thoughts that you encountered throughout the day in the first column. In the second column, you will then identify which cognitive distortion types you're now able to identify from column one. Afterwards, head over to column three and consider all of the factors that make up the scenario that you're stressing over. Try to look at the situation from all angles and look for facts that back up both sides of the argument. Try to challenge the thoughts in column one and write down your now rational and logical argument in column three. You can redo this method however many times you like so as to let out all of your anxious thoughts and worries, then logically work through them in this method.

Similarly, this method can be used for financial issues which you may be worried about. Write down your fears in column one. For instance, you're worried that you aren't investing enough for your later years in life., Work through this method with the necessary research on how to restructure your finances in an efficient way to comfort these fears and rationalize the cognitive distortions.

The method does get a little tricky when it comes to family, relationship and parenting-related issues, because cognitive distortions can stem deeply from family, cultural, traditional or societal pressures which we had to face as we grew up. In adulthood, we start to see these issues come to light as we discover more about ourselves. If you are able to, carefully, gently and safely practice self-awareness (with your triggers in mind), then you can work through the triple column method a few times to assist your mind in logically reframing its thoughts, rationalising the distortions and reducing anxiety. However, if you feel as though visualizing your triggers and exploring cognitive distortions from your triggers can enhance your levels of anxiety, then it may be best to seek help from a mental health professional for the first few times.

Another important key to note to aid in CBT is to gather evidence against your cognitive distortions. You can also self-monitor to pinpoint exactly what you're triggered by as well as what thoughts you encounter when triggered. Journaling can be a fantastic resource to use when self-monitoring, so that you can always go back to past events and pick up on patterns, or simply assess your own thoughts once you've jotted them down. This can be an extremely efficient way for you to pinpoint your own triggers or thought patterns.

Journaling simply involves diarizing the events which occurred throughout the day, your thoughts on them and how you feel overall. Those that journal twice a day often write down their goals and affirmations in the morning, as well as how they feel, and then return to the journal entry in the evening as a way of "checking in" with themselves.

You can also aim to question your thought patterns in your journal, or mentally if you prefer. Some questions which you can ask yourself are:

- Is this thought productive or constructive to the situation I'm facing?
- Am I feeling better or worse from this thought? This question can relate back to the cost-benefit method.
- Can I test the reliability or rationality of this thought? How?
- What evidence is there to back up this thought and is there any evidence counteracting this thought?
- Am I mentally filtering any other information that should be considered in this thought?

These are a few simple questions to help challenge your own thought patterns. If you start to notice a trend in specific negative thoughts or distortions, you can work through the CBT method or the NLP methods to help reframe your thoughts toward a more constructive and positive light.

SEEKING PROFESSIONAL HELP WITH CBT EXERCISES

Although there are various methods to practice re-framing our thoughts and mental distortions, it's understandable that some RNTs and distortions are more deeply rooted than others and may require professional help to identify and reframe our mental maps.

Cognitive restructuring has a lot of promise in combating various issues related to depression, PTSD, anxiety disorders, family/marital issues, substance issues, etc. Therefore, it's understandable that some may need to seek professional help to work through those deeper-rooted thought patterns. Finding a professional may especially be advised if you are dealing with higher levels of trauma.

When seeking professional help, you may have to ask them if they have knowledge of CBT methods to assist you with your thought patterns. It's also important to note that you need to feel comfortable enough with this professional to fully and authentically heal from your past traumas while working through your mental patterns. This relationship is purely based on personal preferences, so try to speak to or see a few professionals before deciding who you feel most comfortable with, because at the end of the day, that will determine how effective the healing process is!

If you're also able to identify specific triggers that affect your cognitive distortion (for instance, dealing with relationships or family issues) then you can use this as a guide to find a counselor that's more specified in this field. In doing so, they can assist you in working through your triggers, identifying their roots and work towards reframing your mental patterns with much more efficiency, and most importantly, it will be done in a safe and measured manner.

Chapter 6

Fourth Technique to Get Motivated in Just One Month

When we speak of taking care of one's mental health, we aren't only referring to managing anxiety and control of one's emotional state. Mental health aims to cover not only bettering our ability to cope within triggering situations, but is a vast term that covers aspects, terms, tools and techniques that assist us in raising our levels of self-awareness and promoting a healthier mind.

Having a healthy mind means creating a constant practice of reducing the stress placed on our brain by finding efficient ways of coping, so as to exercise our minds for a long term healthy brain. As we have come to understand, the stress levels within our lifestyle and diet have all led to an increased risk of contracting disorders (such as anxiety and depression), as well as diseases such as Alzheimer's disease. Rather than letting these stressors and negative emotions get the better of us, we can use tools such as CBT and mindfulness to safeguard our mental health from the risk of disorders and disease.

Mindfulness comes in the form of various cathartic practices such as yoga, meditation, dancing, art, exercising, cooking, writing or reading, etc. However, one of the most powerful forms of mindfulness is meditation because it allows us to quickly and efficiently go within our own mind (and self) to bring our minds and self to a state of peace and relaxation. It allows us to rationally and calmly go about our day and treat every situation with a calm and collected approach. Naturally, in doing so, it reduces our likelihood of our minds turning to cognitive distortions or negative thought habits as an automatic response.

Additionally, meditation also helps reduce symptoms of anxiety (such as fatigue, disrupted sleep cycles and demotivation) by keeping our minds in a constant, calm state throughout the day. In doing so, we aren't wasting energy or triggering negative and draining emotions in situations that don't necessarily require the reaction which we would have once given them. In essence, meditation can help us store our energy and keep it consistent throughout the day.

The power of meditation lies in strengthening our ability to slow down our mind's thoughts and observe the world without judgement. In essence, meditation helps us pay attention and become more present at the moment. In doing so, those who suffer from mental health issues can experience a major reduction in symptoms and achieve feelings of calmness, peace and balance.

The Power of Mindfulness and Meditation

Mindfulness and meditation work hand-in-hand to essentially promote better mental health. Meditation aims to enter a higher state of consciousness so as to promote the idea of "going within," while mindfulness tackles the idea of being present at the moment.

Meditation is such a highly powerful tool because it helps us delve deeper into our own minds and explore areas of our subconscious. In doing so, we're able to identify triggers and thought patterns and help bring them to light so that we can work on them and heal them. Mindfulness helps us to take that healing process one step further by considering how our mental maps and thought patterns influence (and are influenced by) our experiences in the real world. It assists us in taking logical steps to process information so that we can train our minds to become much more efficient when dealing with tough situations. Both mindfulness and meditation practices have proven effects of reducing one's anxiety levels, as it promotes living in the present moment without fear.

The combination of the two factors bred the new movement of mindfulness-based meditation. This practice aimed its focus on those that suffered from anxiety, and designed exercises around treatments for the symptoms of anxiety. Mindfulness-based meditation stems from the mindfulness movement known as Mindfulness-based Stress Reduction (MBSR) that was founded by Jon Kabat-Zinn.

In Zinn's approach, the main goal was to master the art of detaching oneself from anxious thoughts by practicing methods of self-awareness, identifying where tension is held in the body, exploring thinking patterns and managing to tackle heavy, negative or difficult emotions in a safe manner.

THE STEPS TO TAKE

It's important to note that meditation takes a lot of time and practice to be effective. You may not see immediate results in one or two sessions of meditating, and you may not even be able to retain focus in your meditation for the first few sessions. The more that we are able to practice tapping into deeper levels of our subconscious, the easier it gets and naturally, the more powerful and effective it becomes. The first and most important factor to note when starting is that you need to dedicate some time aside for practicing so that you allow yourself to naturally fall into the habit of meditating and reap the benefits (Cuncic, 2020).

1. When you're ready to practice meditation, try to find a comfy spot to sit (either on the floor or on a chair) with your back upright. Ensure that

you are barefoot, with your feet either flat on the floor or in a cross-legged position (ensure that either your buttocks or your feet are touching the floor so as to 'ground' yourself to the earth). It's also important that you find a spot that is quiet, with as little distractions as possible, so that you can concentrate on your meditation much easier.

2. Close your eyes and draw your attention to your breath. Focus on your inhalations and exhalations. If you hear any noises surrounding you, try to block them out and focus on hearing the rhythm of your breathing.

3. Once you've brought your mind and body to a calmer state, explore your thoughts. What is worrying you? What do you fear? Allow these thoughts to unveil themselves so that you can identify and acknowledge them, peacefully.

4. Once you have acknowledged your anxious thoughts, bring your attention back to your breathing and control your inhalations and exhalations. Take deep, long breaths and feel the oxygen flow through your body, from your nostrils through to your shoulders, down to your fingertips and to your toes.

5. Allow the breaths that you take to relax any areas of your body where you once placed tension.

6. Remain in this quiet, calm state for ten more minutes and just focus on your breath healing your body and mind.

7. Once ready, slowly bring your attention back to the room you're in. Take note of the sounds around you, what you feel around you, etc. Gently open your eyes and sit in silence for a few more minutes, allowing yourself to experience the present moment.

You should feel a refreshed, calming sensation when you bring your attention back to the present moment. At first, you may need some extra time to enter your meditation and come out of it (some people feel hazed from the calming effects of it), but this will become much easier to tap in and out of over time! You will also be able to tap into your thought patterns and triggers much quicker, as well as explore them much deeper, the more you practice.

Naturally, creating a habit out of meditating isn't everyone's cup of tea. Some may enjoy it and dive right in, while others may find the practice ineffective, boring or even overwhelming. One thing that we cannot ignore, however, is the effective and powerful benefits of the practice! So for those who are struggling to get into the swing of things, there are a few ways to help you practice meditation. Two of the most important factors to consider are that meditation is a practice that takes time and that, as with any other habit that you're trying to form, you'll need to dedicate time towards it until it's natural. Therefore, you will need to trust the process and have some patience when it comes to getting results from meditation.

Thankfully, due to the movements for mindfulness and meditation, there has been an increase in ways to make meditation more fun and easily accessible for everyone. There are a plethora of guided meditations on streaming sites such as Youtube and Apple Music, which have been created to help walk you through meditations that are specific to your needs (such as healing or reprogramming mental thought habits). There are also mindfulness apps available—which we will explore later in this chapter. There are numerous ways to make meditation a part of your daily routine, it may just take some time to find out which methods work best for you—similar to how you may have to work with a few counselors prior to finding one whom you work well with!

It's also important to note that meditation shouldn't be a strict practice. Some prefer to tackle meditation with a more strict and disciplined approach while others enjoy doing it in their quiet moments without many restrictions. You can also pre-plan meditations based on what you'd like to explore, or simply sit down and bring your mind to a calmer state. It's all completely up to the individual on how they would like to meditate, and what works best for them!

Some stray away from meditation because they feel as though the strictness and levels of discipline required for it add more to their anxiety than not doing it at all. Aim to design a meditation schedule which suits you, as well as a meditation plan that you're interested in working through. One can also try to schedule their meditations for when they're doing other cathartic practices, such as dancing, yoga, painting, etc. Meditation can go hand-in-hand with these activities as well as journaling to help you delve deeper into your thought patterns and cognitive behaviours in a safe and calm environment.

SCHEDULE YOUR DAILY DOSE

With all of the responsibilities that we have to tackle on a day-to-day basis, it's understandable that the idea of taking on one more task may seem overwhelming to us. However, one can argue that the energy and effects that come with meditation *can* help you tackle all of your daily tasks (and maybe even more!) with ease. As meditation helps to promote balanced levels of emotion and energy throughout the day, it also combats the negative emotions and energies which we constantly fight to ward off. For instance, lethargy and demotivation are a few common side effects of anxiety disorder. Regular practice of meditation can help relieve those side effects and reduce levels of anxiety, so as to offer you much more sustainable energy throughout the day.

Therefore, the first few practice runs of meditation may feel a little taxing, but once you start to feel the benefits of meditation, you'll not only be meditating out of habit, but you'll also experience a greater boost in energy and motivational levels! You will also feel much more in control of your emotional state, and with that, feel much more in control of your environment. At the very least, you won't let negative events that you encounter trigger you as much as they once did.

With that in mind, we now need to aim our attention at *how* to go about gaining good momentum in ensuring a consistent and constant practice of meditation. However, diving in the deep end and committing to meditation every day. So, to make it less daunting, let's start small: make it a challenge to meditate every day for one week (Stibich, 2020).

In the first week, aim to set reminders to practice meditation within each day, no matter the length or intensity of the meditation. You can also include mini meditations throughout the day to keep your mind at ease. Mini meditation sessions throughout the day can also help you to break up a long and seemingly daunting hour long meditation for the day into four easy quadrants of quick fifteen-minute sessions! As you move closer to the end of the week, you can try to cluster up those sessions into a dedicated time slot, i.e. dedicating 7pm-8pm for meditation. In this exercise, you're allowing yourself to slowly adjust to a more structured time for meditation, while also subconsciously noting that you can take mini meditations whenever you please!

If the one week exercise doesn't appeal to you,

here are a few other options to consider to help ease you into a more structured meditation cycle:

· Try assigning meditative aspects to a daily chore or activity that you do everyday. For instance, everyone has to wash their dishes, so if you can practice your deep breathing while doing that, then you've already been able to bring your mind and body to a calmer state! Try to find a chore or activity that your body is already used to and doesn't require too much thinking—for instance, if you need to do your laundry and organize your cupboard, this may require a greater amount of your attention. Rather try to choose a chore or activity that your body can automatically tackle via muscle memory, so that you can place your mental focus on meditating. While practicing your breath work, you can also try to bring your attention to your anxious thoughts (when your body and mind are calm enough to explore them) so as to identify them and acknowledge them.

· Walking or exercising are fantastic ways to regulate your breathing while getting your body moving for the day! There is a well-known walking meditation practice (started by Viatnamese monk Thich Nhat Hanh) whereby you take a breath with each step. This meditation practice relies on slow paced walking which forces you to slow down and be present at the moment, while also getting your body moving. Once you've managed to gaat the momentum of one step per breath, you can lengthen each breath and try to have it last two steps, then three, and so forth. This practice is quite similar to the freestyle stroke in swimming, whereby your aim is to take one breath every two or three strokes. The walking meditation practice is quite versatile in the sense that you can practice it wherever you are! In regards to exercising while practicing breath work, you can aim to regulate your breath with each movement. For instance, when lifting weights, you can aim to inhale upon lifting the weight and then exhaling when lowering the weight.

· Another interesting way to practice mindful breathing is to identify sound cues. This practice is commonly and traditionally practiced by monks who would identify a specific sound (such as wind chimes in the temple) and this sound would serve as a notifier to take two deep breaths whenever they heard this sound. You can also use sound cues to take a few seconds worth of a mental pause and bring your attention to the present moment. For instance, you could have a reminder on your phone for every few hours or identify a common sound in your environment and treat that sound as a notifier to take a few deep breaths or a short mental break (by focusing on the present moment).

· Doing a quick session of meditation as a break between activities or places. For instance, meditating after you wake up and eat breakfast or as you come back from work. Meditating in between settings can help rejuvenate and re-energize your mind before you tackle the next task. Rather than feeling tired and lethargic, try to take a quick fifteen-minute meditation break. In this break, you can bring your attention to your breathing, and then take a mental break from your day to acknowledge the stresses of the day, then bring your mind and body back to a core state of calmness. In doing so, you can allow yourself to be much more energized and fully present at the moment, thus boosting your levels of awareness and function optimally.

· The last point is one of the easier methods to take on—it simply requires you to take breaks throughout the day to focus on your breathing, for only two breaths at a time. Bringing our attention back to our breathing throughout the day (by simply taking two deep, mindful breaths) can also help calm and re-energize our bodies and minds at any point in the day. By taking two deep and mindful breaths, one can allow themselves to become more aware of the present moment while reducing the anxiety and tension that's building up within the mind and body.

Although these above exercises aren't necessarily

a full meditation practice, they can greatly help you remain in a calm state while keeping you aware of the present moment. These exercises can be treated as quick methods to reduce anxiety while reaping some of the benefits of mindfulness throughout the day, such as a consistent level of energy and higher levels of concentration. In practicing these exercises, you're developing your "meditation muscles," which can be put to greater use when sitting down for a proper meditation session. These exercises can help you to quickly bring your body to a calm state while also helping you to easily identify and check in on anxious thoughts. For example, if you're aware that a conflict at work has been triggering your levels of anxiety, you can take short meditative breaks throughout the day so as to keep yourself calm. You can then come back to that triggering situation in your proper meditation session later that day to acknowledge the emotions and thoughts, and by doing so, bring peace to the situation.

When you are choosing which meditative practices that you'd like to do, consider exercises that suit your lifestyle. For instance, if you don't exercise regularly, you might want to choose another form of meditation such as the sound cue exercise or the two-breath meditation exercise. If you know that you exercise with a group of people everyday, maybe consider doing the chore meditation practice or the two breath meditation practice, so that you can be alone and with as little distraction as possible.

With all of the versatile options for how to go about practicing mindful meditation, there is truly an opportunity on any occasion to take time aside and bring your mind and body back to a calm state. It's all up to you how you would like to practice—whether it's scheduling fifteen-minute in the morning and evening, or taking little mindful breaks, you can decide which exercises best suit your schedule so as to keep your meditation muscles active!

EXERCISES FOR HEALING

In addition to the exercises that can help you fit meditation into your schedule, there are also a few other ways that you can explore to see which type of exercise and practice appeals to you. For instance, some may find painting to be a cathartic and meditative way to release anxious thoughts, while others may find the activity of painting to make them more anxious and prefer to sit in silence and explore their thoughts. Others may find that they're most at peace while cleaning, while others who despise cleaning might find their most peaceful moments while walking or exercising. It is all up to your personal preferences and what you find most peaceful.

At the end of the day, our aim is to be conscious of these areas of our lives where we can practice mindfulness so that when we do a meditation session, we can easily bring our body to that state of calmness and explore our subconscious.

You can even break these areas of focus into six

simple categories of mindful breathing, observation, awareness, listening, immersion and appreciation ("6 Mindful Exercises You Can Try Today," n.d.). Mindful breathing (as discussed in the previous section) involves taking deep breaths to calm the mind and body down, allowing it to experience the present moment. Deep breathing helps identify where the tension and negative thoughts are held, then helps you acknowledge and release them.

Mindful observation also helps bring your attention to the present moment by placing your focus on a natural object (such as a plant) or other surroundings. This is done by placing all of your focus on that one object for a few minutes and releasing any other thoughts or stimuli that may distract you from focusing. This can help you to expand your levels of concentration as well as balance out your energy levels.

Mindful awareness can help work with cognitive distortions by influencing you to find aspects within your surroundings that you're thankful or appreciative of. This form of mindfulness can be through sensory cues or through intentional thoughts. For instance, if you are looking to use sensory cues for mindful awareness, you can walk out into nature and feel the textures of plants or flowers and think of how they've grown and what they've weathered. This is an example of using your 'touch' sense to bring your awareness back to the present moment. This can also happen with different foods that you taste or sights that you see. With intentional thinking, you can aim to identify your negative thoughts and combat them with positive thoughts in the same situation. For example, if you think that you're dreading how much work you have, you can combat this thought with how grateful you are that you have work to do.

Mindful listening pertains to training your mind and ears to focus on listening in a non-judgmental manner, thus allowing you to fully embrace experiences and encounters before allowing them to affect your emotions and energy. One way of practicing this form of meditation is to listen to new music that you haven't heard before (something new to you) and allow yourself to listen to the tracks without forming any judgements on the music. Embrace the songs, the instruments, the lyrics, etc. and allow the music to take you on a journey without you forming any judgements, biases or labels. Even if you aren't fond of the music at first, allow yourself to get lost in the experience and release any opinions that you may have. The main idea of this exercise is for you to rely on your sense of hearing and fully immerse yourself in that experience, while detaching from your own thoughts.

Mindful immersion revolves around feeling content in the present moment, while calming your mind from future worries, goals and expectations. Our minds are so constantly flooded with thoughts of the past and the future that we barely allow ourselves to fully embrace the present. This exercise promotes bringing your attention *fully* to what you're doing at the moment. For example, if you're taking a walk, embrace the stimuli—what are you seeing, hearing, feeling, etc. This exercise can also be a great and efficient way of grounding yourself.

Mindful appreciation is quite similar to mindful awareness, but a step up. This exercise suggests finding five things within your day that you would usually not notice or appreciate. For example, things that we take for granted, such as our health, a lovely interaction with someone, being able to have a full meal or electricity. We can even simply aim to appreciate the lovely weather or the area that we live in! In doing so, this exercise allows us to boost our own energy levels by combating weighty and draining emotions. Our minds and bodies are so well-adjusted to being on auto-pilot mode and meeting the criteria or requirements for the day, that we often overlook the many small moments which can easily and quickly boost our energy levels and mood!

If you are on the opposite end of the spectrum and enjoy a more structured approach towards your lifestyle and habits, then you can try a few of the exercises that are highlighted in a mindfulness treatment program created by Flemming and Kocovski (Ackerman, 2020). One of the main highlights in their research (which include some of the exercises mentioned in the previous chapter, such as mindfulness awareness, immersion and breath exercises) is the 'raisin' exercises.

The raisin exercise is the first exercise mentioned by Flemming and Kocovski, and is a fantastic starting point for beginners. Although this exercise makes use of a raisin, you can use any food that you prefer. The process works similar to the mindful listening exercise, but in this exercise you will examine a raisin (or food of choice) and act as though this is the first time that you are seeing the food. You will need to pay attention to how the raisin looks, feels, smells and tastes—essentially embracing the experience of seeing this fruit for the first time. In doing so, the exercise helps bring one's attention back to the present moment. Naturally, the more one practices this exercise, the easier it is to hone in on the present moment and be fully aware—as we can also do this exercise on any object, not just a raisin.

Lastly, you can also look at mindfulness apps or guided meditations on streaming services. Mindfulness apps such as Headspace, Reflectly and Calm are readily available on Android and iOS. Headspace allows you to choose and schedule in your own guided meditations for the days, while Reflectly gives you prompts to journal each day (and helps you work through your anxieties), and Calm is a meditation based app which helps you bring your mind to a calmer state prior to sleeping. Reflectly is a great way to logically work through your anxious thoughts and can be compared to the triple column method. The app is so well designed to suit individuals' needs that it can even recommend online therapists to you, or guide you by curating the journal prompts to serve you better. There are also guided meditations which you can find on streaming services such as YouTube, where you can even listen to while you're working or doing other tasks so as to keep your mind in a calm and peaceful state.

With all of the options readily available for you to explore, there truly is a plethora of resources to suit your lifestyle and schedule, especially thanks to the mindfulness movements and current conversations surrounding mental health. We now also have the ability to make use of our phones to remind us to take moments aside and focus on our breath work, taking mindful breaks or simply getting a good walk or stretch in. Considering how near we are to our devices during most of the day, it's become much easier to set reminders and be notified of the breaks we need to take. Once you have gotten your muscles used to the benefits of practicing mindful meditation, we can then work towards dedicating a specific time in the day towards a meditation session. For instance, a session of meditation in the morning or in the evening, prior to sleeping.

CREATING A HEALTHY HABIT OF JOURNALING

Journaling has become a powerful and effective tool that many have adopted to help them process their own thoughts and experiences. Journaling allows you to practice expressing your opinions and emotions through writing so that you can process them objectively later on.

In doing so, journaling provides an extremely efficient way for many to spot their own cognitive distortions and biases, then creates efficient ways of reprogramming their own minds towards a more constructive outlook. Consider the idea of the triple column method—the sentiment within that exercise is one of many exercises that one can practice within journaling.

> *"Whether you're keeping a journal or writing as a meditation, it's the same thing. What's important is you're having a relationship with your mind."*

· Natalie Goldberg

We can also consider journaling a mindfulness exercise, as it allows you a way to release your thoughts, detach from them and then analyze them later on. Many people also like to release their thoughts and emotions in a journal entry and then take a break to meditate a bit (to calm their mind and body) and then come back to the journal entry to re-assess it.

The process of journaling also pushes you to exercise your left brain, the analytical and rational side. However, if you express yourself best through creative means (such as writing poetry or sketching) in your journal, you can also give the right hemisphere of your brain a good workout! Overall, journaling is meant to serve as a cathartic release for you while helping you work through your daily life experiences (Ackerman, 2021).

A few benefits of journaling:

- Promotes a boost in your mood and level of motivation.
- Enhances your sense of well-being.
- Keeps you practicing healthy and rational levels of awareness.
- Keeps you grounded and focused on you, your goals and your healing.
- Reduces symptoms of depression and anxiety (especially directly prior to or directly after a stressful event)
- Can help reduce intrusive thoughts, or at least help you identify intrusive thought patterns and figure out how to reprogram your mental habits to be more beneficial and healthy for you.
- Improves your working memory. In doing so, it reduces the risk level of neurodegenerative diseases at a later stage in life.
- Can also help you to spot unhealthy habits and find creative and effective ways of breaking those old habits and replacing them with new ones. For instance, if you're looking to start a new diet and reduce your intake of fast food, you can journal your experience while exploring different diets as well as your relationship with different foods. This point can be considerably helpful for those instances where you need to seek professional help. The professional can then assess your journal entries to best under-

stand your situation. This habit can be useful in many other scenarios as well—such as logging your sleep cycles if you struggle with regular and quality sleep.

The first step to journaling is to explore a few different methods and see which style you prefer in relation to your lifestyle. For instance, if you'd enjoy using an app (such as Reflectly) it can remind you to journal, as well as prompt you to reflect on the day. You can also be creative with your journaling practice to suit your style—for instance, journaling doesn't need to necessarily only be expressed through coherent written sentences. You can use keywords, poetry, sketches or even quotes from others to best express yourself. And if you are worried about writer's block, don't worry! There are a variety of journal prompt exercises that you can find online. You can even turn to social media hashtags such as "JournalPrompts" or "Journaling" to help you find prompts. These social media hashtags can additionally help you to establish or join a community to keep you motivated and creative as you journal!

In terms of creating a habit out of journaling, it can be introduced similarly to how you would introduce meditation into your day—you should ideally start by dedicating at least a few minutes in the evening to reflect on your day. Later, try to start journaling a bit in the morning, too. The morning journal entries could include how you slept, what you have to do today, if you have any worries or anxieties for the day's tasks as well as a few positive affirmations and goals. You can then refer back to your journal in the evening. In the evening journal entry, you can include reflection on the day as well as reflect back on the morning's journal entry to see how your day went. Keep in mind, it's alright to have good and bad days as well as productive and non-productive days! The goal is to be as aware, authentic and as present as possible. If you're journaling without honesty, it will not be productive and will inhibit your growth!

When creating the habit of journaling, you should also aim to make it as enjoyable as possible for you. While the exercise may be a serious one and feel taxing at times, it's there to help you. Therefore, aim to at least make the process enjoyable for you. Plus, when you're enjoying the process, the more you'll learn and want to explore for yourself. Making journaling enjoyable is all up to you—whether it's incorporating colours or symbols into your entries, or adding song lyrics or funky photos (similar to a scrapbook vibe).

Another important way to make journaling fun is to set goals and compliment yourself when you reach achievements or things that you're excited about. And don't only aim to use the journal for serious matters, such as goals and working through emotional problems, aim to also include the fun and happy moments into your journal! Let's take the general workflow in a company as an example. The company will have requirements for you, like setting goals and deadlines for work and you may experience many challenges along the way. However, the company can't expect you to work for them and meet their goals without re-imbursing you as well as maybe even offering some incentives, such as employee of the month, along the way. Similarly, you can't expect yourself to consistently be chasing goals and working without rewarding yourself and acknowledging the accomplishments you've done!

These incentives, compliments and affirmations are so vital to keeping one's motivation and energy levels up, as well as protecting your own state of mental health. These good factors are there to remind you to stay focused on the goals and accomplishments along the way.

As you slowly start to develop a regular habit of journaling and have found your preferred methods of journaling, we can then move onto a more methodical manner of journaling so that you can reap the most benefits out of the practice.

Journaling needs to be something extremely personal—you need to work towards being comfortable being fully open and vulnerable in your journal. Therefore, to ensure that you're able to fully focus on your journal entries, consider the environment and atmosphere that you're in. The space needs to be quiet and free of distractions. You should also aim to journal during the least stressful period of your day. This is not to say that you shouldn't journal when you are stressed—you can use your journal whenever you'd like. However, you should also dedicate and prioritize some time within your day to journal so that you can fully focus on your thoughts and emotions.

Next, aim to slowly ease yourself into what you would like to journal about. If you want to journal about a past trauma that you faced, for instance, don't force yourself into journaling about it straight away. Think of each journal entry as a coffee catch-up with someone that you trust. You wouldn't necessarily dive right into all of the deep details without asking that person how they are and having a little lighthearted banter first, right? Treat your journal entries similarly. Ease yourself into the entry by journaling about your day, how you feel, or even recounting something as small as the weather that day. Allow yourself to ease into the writing process and let the deeper thoughts flow through your mind and onto the paper. If you rush into it, you may be influenced to simply copy down the event, thought or trigger without fully exploring it and questioning it.

Once you've managed to adjust to the habit of journaling, figure out how to make it enjoyable for yourself and dedicate blocks of time to journal; you can then move on to practicing and refining the structure in your journal entries. The structure is so important in your entries because it can make it much easier for you to analyze your own entries and identify areas that you'd like to improve upon. However, structuring your entries will come naturally and with time. The structure of journal entries can also be personalized—think of it as an artist's signature touch, which develops and is refined over time.

Lastly, it's only fair that we end this section with an acronym to help us remember to journal; and naturally, that acronym is: What topic, Review/Reflect, Investigate, Time yourself, and Exit smart (WRITE). This acronym and guideline was provided by the Center for Journal Therapy and offers an effective way to the process of combining CBT with journaling.

- "What topic" refers to what you would like to write about. This step essentially allows you to have a starting point or central point for your journal entry. Say, for instance, that you would like to journal about work today—give that topic a central point and headline (such as 'Work') and write it down. From there, you can then elaborate on that topic, explaining the scenario, your feelings towards it, factors that influenced it, how you may have coped, etc.
- "Review/Reflect" is simple. This step refers to taking a few moments to calm yourself (by meditating, taking a break or simply stepping away from the journal for a few moments to have a mental distraction from the journaling process) then returning to the entry to reflect upon it. The reflection/review can also be a new journal entry or a sub-category of the same journal entry. Aim to start your review section with sentences such as "I feel," "I want," "I think," and

"I aim." These sorts of statements allow you to positively critique your entries without judgement. You should also aim to keep the reflection entries in the present tense so as to promote growth and healing. Using words in your statements such as "right now," "today," and "currently," can greatly help you put the journal entry into perspective. It can help you understand that this is just a small period in your life and that your healing, worth and growth is endless.

· "Time" revolves around dedicating a certain amount of time to journaling. You can use a timer or alarm to help you ensure that you're spending the right amount of time for each journaling session. At first, you may feel like five minutes of journaling is an eternity, and then a few weeks down the line, you may feel as though you could do ten of those five-minute journaling sessions and it still wouldn't be enough! Dedicating time to journaling can greatly help you prioritize *just* focusing on expressing yourself without any distractions. It also forces you to fill up that time space with the exploration of your thoughts. Have you heard of the phrase "I guess I'll be sitting alone with my thoughts then"? This is exactly what we *want* to do when we refer to dedicating time to journaling. We want to be alone with our thoughts so that we can explore all of the corners of our minds and work on more efficient ways of processing our experiences and thoughts! Setting time aside to journal will soon become part of your daily habits. When that happens, you will naturally be able to fill your journal entry sufficiently within the time frame that you have given yourself.

· "Exit" is the last step within this acronym, and it's quite a fitting term for the last step! This refers to creating a strategic exit plan with good introspection and a dedication to work on what you have written thus far. If you would like to neatly end your journal entry, you can add a concise conclusion sentence. Try to keep the conclusion as constructive as possible with a touch of positivity at the end. For example, you can end the entry by starting the conclusion with words along the lines of "I am starting to notice that," "I am now aware that," or "I plan on," "I am working on," "I see that..." and then make mention of areas that you would like to acknowledge (these could be strength areas that you'd like to highlight or areas that you would like to work on). Afterwards, leave yourself a little motivating end sentence to get you excited for healthy and positive change! This could be a little "you can do it!", or a "well done today." Anything that you feel may motivate you to keep on pushing, healing, learning and growing.

The "exit" step is also similarly related to the last

step in meditation, when you have to work on bringing yourself back to the present moment. The exit strategy allows you to make peace and accept what has happened, and then bring your awareness back to the present moment. This is done so that you don't spend too much time thinking on past events or fixating on the entry. It allows your mind and energy levels to be grounded and brought back to the present moment, releasing all the stress and anxieties of the day.

This guided step-by-step acronym can be helpful towards refining your perfect journal experience. Once you have gotten to this step you will start to experience major improvements in your levels of energy due to the efficiency with which you process events. Remember, healing is an ongoing process and you need to treat all of these exercises (as well as your own healing) with patience, love and awareness. These are all tools to help you and you will naturally become more efficient with the tools and techniques the more you practice them and adopt them as habits.

Chapter 7

Fifth Technique to Break Bad Habits

As we have come to learn through this book, we have both bad and good habits within us. One of the most debilitating bad habits is that of negative thinking, which we have managed to target and combat with reprogramming, CBT and meditation. However, it doesn't stop there. Many lifestyle habits can also fuel negative thoughts rather than combat them—for instance, eating too much fast food can leave us feeling lethargic, demotivated and can quite often lead to episodes of depression or anxiety.

Naturally, as we aim to better our mental health, we should then also aim to adjust lifestyle habits that can lead to a deterioration in mental health. The best health (physically and mentally) stems from a consistent approach and balance within all aspects of our lives—this includes social, financial, nutritional, and physical. By restricting or over-indulging in certain factors of our lifestyle, we neglect other aspects that are so vitally important to promote a healthy, happy brain and body.

One may argue that they have no other choice but to live a lifestyle where certain aspects require much more attention than others, and that they have no choice but to neglect other aspects in the process (such as nutrition, recreational or social aspects). However, if one is leading a lifestyle that is more demanding in one area, rather than promoting balance to all aspects of a lifestyle, then that means that one will have to acknowledge this dilemma and try to find creative ways of incorporating those other factors into their lifestyle. This doesn't necessarily mean that work has to be compromised, but it promotes the notion that one's quality of life and mental health needs to be much more protected so as to handle such demanding aspects. In layman's terms, one will need to find ways of bringing a more healthy balance into their lifestyle so that they have the energy, motivation and mental capacity to tackle that demanding aspect of life.

Another example is that if you feel that your responsibilities lie heavily within your household and your children or family, then you will need to find creative ways to break bad habits and replace them with ones that promote healthy balance and sustainable energy. For instance, rather than going out to drink with friends to escape from the responsibilities at home, rather try to balance this out by going for a jog and practicing half an hour of mindfulness so that you can tackle the responsibilities at home.

One way of testing whether your habit is promoting good or bad mental health patterns and keeping you stuck in a vicious cycle of exhaustion is to be aware of the after-effects of that habit. Ask whether this habit is helping you feel more prepared to tackle those responsibilities, or whether the habit is keeping you stuck in a constant cycle of trying to cope with the stress. Bad habits can be associated with negative thoughts—they are draining and leave you feeling more demotivated than before, especially in regards to tackling all of your responsibilities or tasks for the day.

A few of the more common forms of bad habits that we experience include poor posture, indulging in fast food and processed food, overuse of social media and technological devices, a lack of physical exercise, codependency, turning to substances to cope, and unhealthy sleep cycles (The Ten Worst Habits for Your Mental Health, n.d.). It's important to note that it's completely normal for us to slip into these bad habits every once in a while; however, overdoing it becomes a gateway for poor mental health to breed.

Breaking Bad Habits

One of the most common habits that many suffer from is irregular sleep cycles. Ironically enough, irregular sleeping habits and GAD do go hand-in-hand. You may suffer from irregular sleep cycles or poor quality of sleep due to GAD, or suffer from more severe symptoms of GAD because of irregular sleep cycles. Understandably, poor quality of sleep can also greatly influence our moods, thought patterns, productivity, cognitive function and overall quality of life.

On average, adults should be aiming to get at least 7 to 8 hours of quality sleep per night so as to allow our minds and bodies to reset for the next day. One of the best ways to achieve a good night's sleep is by calming the mind and its thoughts. Through mindful meditation before bed, one can be able to ward off any negative or anxious thoughts, then bring oneself to a calm enough state so as to get in a good quality of sleep. The Calm and Headspace apps are great apps to use for this purpose, as they have narrated stories with calming music to help ease the mind into a more relaxed state. One can also adjust their sleep schedule to try and go to bed 15 minutes earlier each night until they manage to correct their cycle and get a good 7 to 8 hours of sleep.

Side effects of poor sleep quality can also include higher risks of neurodegenerative diseases. Therefore, caring for one's sleep cycle is vitally important for short-term and long term mental and physical health.

Another bad habit that's extremely common is inactivity. The mind and body both need an outlet to reduce stress and keep active. Exercising is a fantastic way to combat the effects of that stress. It's notable to add that less than 5% of adults in the United States achieve the minimum requirement of 30 minutes of physical exercise per day ("How to Break Bad Habits Caused By Anxiety," n.d.). Whether we dedicate this half an hour each day to a light stroll or a yoga session, it can greatly benefit both the mind and body in promoting sustainable energy throughout the day. One can also aim toward adding in a meditative session while on a walk or in a yoga session in order to ground yourself while getting in your physical movement for the day.

Whether you're trying to cut down on fast food, regulate your sleep cycle or reduce your reliance on substances, objects or people (through codependency), the best way to go about this is to first meditate on that habit to see what it stems from. For example, you may be eating more fast food because you feel as though you have no time to cook after work. Once you've been able to find the triggers for these bad habits, you can then go on to tackle evolving that habit in a slow and controlled way. Remember, effective change doesn't happen overnight; so allow yourself to slowly adjust and ease yourself out of the old habits that leave you feeling drained or out of control of your own life.

Good Habits to Adopt

To replace old habits, or simply to adopt and incorporate more productive and positive habits into our lifestyles, the first step is dedication and scheduling. Whether it's a mere two minutes out of each day or simply scheduling the habit near to a daily event (such as lunch), one can easily practice incorporating good habits into their lifestyle!

Similar to how we aimed at introducing meditation practices into our daily schedule, this can be done with other lifestyle habits that can also boost our energy levels, motivation as well as promote better physical health! Aside from the two habits of meditating and practicing breath work, one can also consider: drinking enough water throughout the day, taking light walks or stretches in between work sessions, stopping yourself to think prior to reacting to a situation, taking the time to observe things objectively or from another person's perspective, practicing appreciation, avoiding stimulants or reducing codependency and managing your expectations. Another way of incorporating good habits into your daily lifestyle is to practice the art of contentment with the present as well as practicing gratitude and positivity. An extremely quick and powerful way to practice these techniques is to either write down a list of things that you're happy about, or create a positive mantra (such as a positive affirmation) to repeat to yourself. In doing so, you'll be able to raise your own energy levels without relying on anything other than the power of your own mind.

Another extremely simple way to practice inner peace and happiness is to practice consciously smiling more often. Similar to the idea that one can fake laughter until they start to genuinely laugh, practicing a smile has amazing physiological effects on our levels of energy (25 Habits to Have in Life, n.d). When we slouch or frown, our minds can take these physiological cues and build on them; similarly, if we practice good posture and smile more often, that effect can turn inward and trick our minds into finding more reasons to smile!

As we have covered, eating fast foods or processed food regularly has a negative effect on our mental health. This is purely down to the notion that our digestive system is considered our body's second brain. Whatever we consume has direct effects on what and how we think. Additionally, foods that aren't easy to process and digest can leave us feeling lethargic, drained and often uncomfortable. One way to combat the constant intake of unhealthy foods is to prepare our stomach for the day by enjoying a healthy and wholesome breakfast (so that our digestive system is at least prepared for whatever else we may consume throughout the day). Millions of Americans skip this meal each day, even though it is the most important one to have. If you struggle to wake up early enough to eat, prepare your meal the night before. If you struggle to eat in the morning, try to slowly introduce your stomach to healthy foods in the morning, such as fibre and fruits.

Lastly, set realistic goals for yourself everyday. In creating micro-goals, we're allowing ourselves the opportunity to achieve some tasks for the day that are realistic and leave us feeling positive about the day. These goals can even be small tasks that help us achieve bigger and greater accomplishments. For instance, create a goal of practicing five minutes of meditation each day. By doing so, you're prioritizing all aspects of your life and not just work or important events. You're prioritizing the habits that you'd like to include in your balanced lifestyle. These habits can even be as simple as going for a walk or drinking enough. At the end of the day, you want to achieve a balanced day where you have been able to look after yourself in all aspects, from work to health. This allows you to push yourself into a good and positive state of mind filled with sustainable energy and motivation!

Chapter 8

Conclusion

From reducing symptoms of anxiety disorder and eliminating negative thoughts, to reprogramming your thought habits through CBT and mindfulness, you can completely reform your mind and lifestyle within a month!

One of the key points to consider with creating new habits (whether it involves mental reprogramming or physical lifestyle changes) is that habits need to go hand-in-hand with the constant practice of self-awareness. It is also important to note that habits need time and patience to develop properly, as with any form of authentic healing.

With this process, we aimed to tackle reformation in five stages: identifying negative thoughts, training your brain to think more positively and rationally through the process of self-awareness, identifying and understanding the habits of cognitive distortions, combating negative thoughts through meditation and mindfulness, and lastly, breaking bad habits and adopting new, constructive habits.

By the end of the five steps, you will stop orbiting around negative thoughts and self-talk and instead be able to detach from them while also gravitating towards positive and healthier modes of thinking and living.

As you move forward in life, it's important to note that there is no limit to self-improvement and that these techniques can serve as lifelong tools to help you consistently and healthily assess yourself, ground yourself, and grow. Habits such as practicing self-awareness, mindfulness, meditation, CBT, breath techniques can always be re-assessed and re-adjusted to help you deal with new experiences that you encounter. These techniques aren't only here to help you heal from past traumas, but can be constantly practiced in order to prevent the build-up of negative thoughts and habits in the future.

You can consider these tools as an immunity booster against viruses in the body—although it may not entirely prevent you from experiencing negative scenarios or even a build-up of anxiety and stress; these tools and techniques are here to help reduce the effects of them on your mind and body, while also helping to healthily cope with these encounters.

Now that you have all of the options readily available at your fingertips, the change can start today! If you are still worried about that first step—you're already there! You have managed to identify your own thoughts and now you have the tools to further explore them, acknowledge them, heal and grow from them.

Allow yourself the patience and time that it takes to heal and explore your mind. Aim to question every thought, behaviour, opinion and reaction you have so that you can test to see if there is a more productive or efficient way of handling it. With all this in mind, take these techniques and tools as means to help you heal. Don't put pressure on yourself to see growth or constantly look for signs of healing and change. Instead, allow the process to take its time and work for you. Have fun with the techniques, be patient and allow yourself to simply embrace the process of healing, and let the signs of growth show themselves in due time!

Chapter 9

References

20 Habits That Make Your Anxiety Worse. The Active Times. (2018, August 24). https://www.theactivetimes.com/healthy-living/20-habits-make-your-anxiety-worse.

22 Mindfulness Exercises, Techniques & Activities For Adults (+ PDF's). PositivePsychology.com. (2020, October 16). https://positivepsychology.com/mindfulness-exercises-techniques-activities/.

6 Mindfulness Exercises You Can Try Today. Pocket Mindfulness. (2017, October 27). https://www.pocketmindfulness.com/6-mindfulness-exercises-you-can-try-today/.

Ackerman. (2021, February 5). *83 Benefits of Journaling for Depression, Anxiety, and Stress.* PositivePsychology.com. https://positivepsychology.com/benefits-of-journaling/.

Adams, R. L. (2019, March 11). *25 Best Habits to Have in Life.* Entrepreneur.

https://www.entrepreneur.com/slideshow/
299317#2.

Adams, R. L. (2019, March 11). *25 Best
Habits to Have in Life*. Entrepreneur.
https://www.entrepreneur.com/slideshow/
299317#3.

Anxiety and Depression Association of America, ADAA. Facts & Statistics | Anxiety and Depression Association of America, ADAA.
https://adaa.org/about-adaa/press-room/facts-statistics.

Cuncic, A. (2020, December 10). *The Benefits of Meditation for Generalized Anxiety Disorder*. Verywell Mind.
https://www.verywellmind.com/the-benefits-of-meditation-for-generalized-anxiety-disorder-4143127.

Faubion, D. (2017, June 5). *Best Affirmations For Anxiety*. BetterHelp. https://www.betterhelp.com/advice/anxiety/best-affirmations-for-anxiety/.

How to Turn Negative Thoughts into Positive Affirmations. Simply Well Coaching. (2019, September 11). https://www.simplywellcoaching.com/blog/are-you-a-bully-how-to-turn-your-negative-thoughts-into-positive-actions/.

Hurst. (2020, February 5). *5 Automatic Negative Thought Examples And How To Overcome Them*. The Law Of Attraction.

https://www.thelawofattraction.com/automatic-negative-thought/.

Learn to Identify Automatic Negative Thoughts. Exploring your mind. (2019, April 23). https://exploringyourmind.com/learn-to-identify-automatic-negative-thoughts/.

MediLexicon International. *Anxiety: Symptoms, types, causes, prevention, and treatment.* Medical News Today. https://www.medicalnewstoday.com/articles/323454.

MediLexicon International. *How to calm anxiety: 8 tips and tricks.* Medical News Today. https://www.medicalnewstoday.com/articles/326115.

MediLexicon International. *Neuro-linguistic programming (NLP): Does it work?* Medical News Today. https://www.medicalnewstoday.com/articles/320368.

Melemis, I. W. to C. M. L. *Cognitive Behavioral Therapy Guide, Free CBT Worksheet, Thought Record.* I Want to Change My Life. https://www.iwanttochangemylife.org/cbt/cognitive-behavioral-therapy-guide.htm#negative-.

Melemis, S. *Cognitive Behavioral Therapy Guide, Free CBT Worksheet, Thought Record.* I Want to Change My Life. https://www.iwanttochangemylife.org/cbt/cognitive-behavioral-therapy-guide.htm#negative-.

NLP Swish Pattern - How To Do It!

https://www.personal-development-planet.com/nlp-swish-pattern.html.

NLP Swish Technique. Pegasus NLP. (2019, April 28). https://nlp-now.co.uk/nlp-swish-technique.

The Reason You Need to Practice Daily Affirmations. Jack Canfield. (2019, December 2). https://www.jackcanfield.com/blog/practice-daily-affirmations/.

Rhode, J. (2020, October 18). *20 Positive Affirmations for Anxiety, Uncertainty, & Fear*. travelJewels. https://www.traveljewels.net/wellness/positive-affirmations-for-anxiety-uncertainty-fear.

Sey, R (n.d.). Positive Thinking: Change Your Thinking and Change Your Life.

Smith, E.-M. *What is Negative Thinking? How It Destroys Your Mental Health*. HealthyPlace. https://www.healthyplace.com/self-help/positivity/what-is-negative-thinking-how-it-destroys-your-mental-health.

Steber, C. (2016, June 30). *11 Tips For More Positive Self-Talk Every Day*. Bustle. https://www.bustle.com/articles/169608-11-tips-for-more-positive-self-talk-every-day.

Stibich, M. *6 Ways to Fit Your Meditation Practice Into Your Day*. Verywell Mind.

https://www.verywellmind.com/how-to-fit-meditation-into-your-day-every-day-2224118.

Sussex Publishers. (2011, August 15). *5 Steps to Make Affirmations Work for You*. Psychology Today. https://www.psychologyto-day.com/us/blog/the-wise-open-mind/201108/5-steps-make-affirmations-work-you.

The Ten Worst Habits for Your Mental Health. CareersinPsychology.org |. (2019, January 3). https://careersinpsychology.org/ten-worst-habits-mental-health/.

These 4 NLP techniques could change how you think. happiness.com. (2020, December 16). https://www.happiness.com/magazine/personal-growth/nlp-happiness-techniques/.

These Bad Habits Are Making Your Anxiety Even Worse. Showbiz Cheat Sheet. (2018, May 10). https://www.cheatsheet.com/health-fitness/bad-habits-making-your-anxiety-worse.html/.

U.S. National Library of Medicine. *PubMed*. National Center for Biotechnology Information. https://pubmed.ncbi.nlm.nih.gov/.

Use NLP to Obliterate Negative Thoughts, Feelings. Tambuli Media. (2019, May 29). https://tambulimedia.com/use-nlp-to-obliter-ate-negative-thoughts-and-feelings/.

WebMD. (2020, June 25). *Anxiety Disorders: Types, Causes, Symptoms, Diagnosis, Treat-*

ment. WebMD. https://www.webmd.com/anxiety-panic/guide/anxiety-disorders%231.

What Lifestyle Changes are Recommended for Anxiety and Depression? Taking Charge of Your Health & Wellbeing. https://www.takingcharge.csh.umn.edu/what-lifestyle-changes-are-recommended-anxiety-and-depression.

Wolff, C. (2016, November 1). *11 Habits Of Calm People That Keep Them Relaxed & In Control Of Their Emotions.* Bustle. https://www.bustle.com/articles/192247-11-habits-of-calm-people-that-keep-them-relaxed-in-control-of-their-emotions.

www.ingramcontent.com/pod-product-compliance
Lightning Source LLC
Chambersburg PA
CBHW032145020426
42334CB00016B/1240